Mary Cook

In My Mind's Eye

www.creativebound.com

Published by Creative Bound Inc.
Box 424, Carp, Ontario
Canada K0A 1L0
(613) 831-3641

ISBN 0-921165-75-7
Printed and bound in Canada

Book design by Wendelina O'Keefe
Cover images © PhotoDisc 2001
Author photo © Roger Sands MPA

National Library of Canada Cataloguing in Publication Data

Cook, Mary, 1932-
    In my mind's eye

ISBN 0-921165-75-7

1.   Cook, Mary, 1932- —Anecdotes. 2. Renfrew (Ont. : County)—
History—Anecdotes. I. Title.

FC3095.R4C65 2001   971.3'8104'092   C2001-903645-0
F1059.R4C65 2001

*S*ilent partners are often the lifeblood of a business or venture. Although they tend to stay in the background, they nonetheless are always there when their help is needed.

I too have had a silent partner throughout my career. Without him, I doubt I could have been a broadcaster for forty-five years; nor could I have churned out thousands of articles for newspapers and magazines, and written eight books. This silent partner has dealt with all the idiosyncrasies adherent to people in my profession, and he has done it with patience and gentle guidance.

My life partner, my husband Wally, with whom I have shared laughter and tears for almost fifty years, has been the steadying rock who has allowed me the freedom I needed to pursue the career which has brought me so much joy.

I know he has made this journey easier by his presence in my life, and so it is with love and gratitute that I dedicate this book to my husband, J. Wallace Cook.

Contents

Introduction

My mother used to say I came into the world with a furrowed brow. As I passed from being a child to adulthood, I worried about everything and everyone. I stewed for days over something as simple as wondering if the meals I prepared for my family included the five food groups from *Canada's Food Guide*. I worried myself sick if a column I wrote had a misplaced verb or I had left out a semicolon. I worried that I had spoken too harshly to one of my children, or had forgotten to say goodbye to my husband as he headed off to work. I even stewed over something as simple as not having the time in my day to do all the things I had written on my 'must do' list.

One day I was lamenting to a good friend how I was worried about something, which was so important I have long since forgotten what is was. What Amy said to me changed for life my attitude about worry. She looked at me for the longest moment and half smiled. It's amazing how I can remember that look but have forgotten what I was so worried about. She said, "Mary, ten years from now, what will it matter?" What will it matter indeed!

I am not going to say I have eliminated all worry from my life. What I am going to say is that I no longer worry about things that won't alter the course of the world or affect my family. I now try to worry only about things that to me are *really* important. Things like my children's and grandchildren's health, and the general well-being of those who are near and dear to me. When you get right down to it, nothing else in life is really all that important.

This change in attitude did not come gradually. It came suddenly after my friend made that profound comment to me. I can remember the day, shortly after our talk, when I first put her philosophy about worry into action.

We were having one of those winter days for which the Ottawa Valley is famous—wind howling, snow blowing, the temperatures below what I call humane. My husband and three children, in spite of the outside elements, had left early that day for the ski hills. I was concerned about the roads and the bad weather and was relieved to see them, skis in tow, at the back door when the day was over. Our house had a large entrance, and on those walls some of my most prized antique plates were displayed. Someone braced their skis against the wainscotting, and before anyone could save them, the skis fell to the floor taking four of my prized plates with them.

I fetched the broom and the dustpan and swept the shards into the garbage. One daughter said, "Mommy, aren't you upset?" I told her I would miss having those familiar plates on the wall, but the most important thing to me was that my family had arrived home safely. Plates I can replace. Children and husband I can't.

This is not to say I no longer get upset. I do. But I try very hard to separate the important issues from those that don't amount to more than a hill of beans.

As I get older I find joy all around me. I can get the utmost enjoyment from something as ordinary as watching two squirrels fighting over a tossed peanut on the front lawn. Contentment can come from doing nothing more exciting that rereading my children's baby books, written when I was a young mother, or just simply braiding grass, a hobby I learned as a child. I guess you could say that over the years I have relearned how to enjoy the simple pleasures I once knew growing up on a farm in Renfrew County.

Long after those Depression years have dimmed, there remains in all of us who are a product of that era, a sense of belonging to a special time in history. For all of us, there will always be reminders of that age in the deepest recesses of our minds. The smell of pine trees, the dankness of a stable, the crust on a snow-covered field, a discarded fender of an old car once used as a toboggan. The memory list is endless. As well, the Depression years gave us a legacy of honesty and integrity. This was a time when deals were made with the shake of a hand. It was an era when a person's word was his bond. A man succeeded or failed by the sweat from his own brow. But above all, these were the years when family, neighbours and community held the country together.

So once again, I invite you to come back with me, back to that time which has been called 'Canada's most terrible years.' These are the stories and memories as seen through the eyes of a child. A child who tried to understand the worries of her parents who strove to raise a family through this difficult period. To *this* child, however, the 1930s were filled with what seemed to be common joys and sorrows of everyday life. Tales of school friends, neighbours and family, when woven together, leave lasting memories that to this day still stir the heart.

Writing and broadcasting these memories have brought me much pleasure over the years. I hope you enjoy taking this trip back with me in time, yet again...

Home

I think I would make a good charwoman. I love a clean house, and although I don't consider myself a fanatic, I do like things orderly. This probably has a lot to do with the fact that as a very young child, when I was too little to reach the cupboard in the kitchen, I stood on a chair and dried dishes. I was expected to do regular cleaning chores every Saturday, and because I was the youngest, I was given what my mother thought were easy tasks, but what I thought were downright awful. The fact is that from the time I was very young, I was expected to contribute to the running of our house on the farm. Mother always said if a job was worth doing, it was worth doing right. I also know that I often had the urge to tell her that I didn't think a certain job was worth doing at all, but of course, that would cut no ice with a mother in the 1930s. A child was expected to do what she was told, do it willingly, and do it right!

No doubt this early indoctrination into home management would turn off most girls, but in my case, the opposite was true. I got to love housework. The days when my sister Audrey and I switched chores with our three brothers, with Mother putting them into long white pinnies in the kitchen and sending us girls to the barns, I longed to be back in the house doing "girl" chores. If it seems strange that the boys in our family were expected to take their turn at household chores, I would like you to know that I think Mother invented the Woman's Movement. She could see nothing wrong with my brothers scrubbing floors, pounding down bread and churning butter. Of course, we couldn't talk about this at the Northcote School, because the boys dreaded being teased about wearing pinnies and doing household chores. The whole business was done on the quiet.

I would like to say that, later on, I carried on the idea of dividing household duties between my son and two daughters, but somewhere along the road I lost my own mother's instinct to divide all chores evenly between the boys and the girls. It had more than a little to do with the fact that there was no barn to send the girls to. Our son worked with his father at chores in which our daughters had little interest, such as driving the truck, installing roller blinds and lugging huge rolls of carpet. Although the girls worked in our department store from the time they were in early grade school, our son never did cotton on to doing housework.

Our daughters hated the lists I made out every Saturday and tacked to the bulletin board in the kitchen, lining out their duties at home before they went to our store to work. These chores included everything from cleaning toilets to vacuuming right through the house. Only this year, long after they were married and had homes of their own, did I learn that they pulled a hazy on me by only vacuuming every second stair and dumping blue cleanser into the toilet bowl and never bothering to swish it around. So much for my efforts to teach them the rudiments of housekeeping.

Although the Depression years were hard years for our parents, never once did we go hungry. Although there was no money for such niceties as fancy dishes and store-bought curtains, Mother went out of her way to bring cheer and brightness to that old log house, which from the outside looked pretty simple and homely. Every occasion was cause for a celebration, and even though there wasn't an ounce of Irish blood in any of us, on St. Patrick's Day the kitchen table was festooned with green cardboard four-leaf clovers and always there were cupcakes with bright green icing for dessert. From the earliest sign of fall, small pumpkins, gourds and, eventually, waxed maple leaves took the plainness away from the sparsely furnished room, and brought life to our table.

This habit carried over into my own marriage. We could have something as simple as homemade stew and a slice of bread for our evening meal, but we always had candles, which my children talk about to this day.

Similarly, when our three children were young, mealtime was a time to talk about our day. It was a time to laugh, a time to lament about the injustice of life as a shy teenager, and a time to exchange ideas and talk about the news of the day. I look back with fondness at these special warm memories of another time.

When parents have to meet the challenge of gearing down when their children go out into the world to make their own way, home and what it stands for takes on a whole new meaning. What was at one time important, doesn't seem to matter all that much anymore. Space becomes a burden instead of a necessity. Rooms once full of stuffed animals, sleeping bags, piggybanks and children's books, long since put on a top shelf, are now trappings that you have to get rid of. They wouldn't fit into the smaller house you are going to move to, and shockingly, your children aren't the least bit interested in cluttering up their homes with the articles from their younger years. So much for sentimentality.

So home becomes a smaller place. Gone are the big spacious rooms, the rolling backyard and the house big enough so that everyone has his or her own space. You try to juxtapose the past with the present by putting up old pictures in your new quarters, and hanging the same curtains and using the same bedspreads, but you think home will probably never be the same again.

Then, never missing a beat, the children and *their* children descend on your new, confined space. The walls bulge, the floor becomes seating space, and sleeping bags for grandchildren compensate for the lack of beds. You come to the heartwarming realization that home is what and where you make it. It has nothing to do with size, trappings or location but has everything to do with continuing on with what you have done all your life—making whatever space you have a place of refuge and a place for family.

When I think about the warmth that emanated from that old log house in the country, I lose sight of the fact that the doors were drafty and the silver-painted stovepipe snaking through the upstairs provided the only heat. All I can visualize is a very cozy and comfortable place.

Happy memories have a way of crowding out those that may have an unpleasantness about them. These stories of the home I knew as a young child are a reflection of an era when a contented home was just as important as a good meal on the table. They are meant to please the reader and enlighten those who were raised after those Depression years. These are the stories of that warm haven of my childhood. They are the stories of my home.

Starving

Father said it was a poor farmer indeed who could not feed his family. He had much more confidence than I did in the ability of the farm to keep food on our table. Every year, when winter was waning, I would find myself once again sinking into the agonies of wondering where our next meal would be coming from.

I knew that the winter was coming to an end. I also knew there was a span of time between winter and when our garden would be grown and producing vegetables, and this fact gave me great concern. I would chance a look into the pork barrel and find that most of those big salted pieces put down in fall would be gone. There would be more empty hooks than full ones in the smokehouse, and I could no longer reach down to the sauerkraut in the bottom of the barrel. I really began to worry when my trips to the cellar showed me that the vegetables buried in the sand were harder and harder to find. I knew it would just be a matter of time until we all starved to death!

I was astonished that no one else shared my fears. Mother and Father, always so practical, seemed oblivious to what I considered an established fact, that our winter stores were getting more scant by the day. I would worry about what was to happen to us. Would some of us have to go to the poorhouse like the old woman on the Barr Line? She had no money and was obliged to live off the county. The very thought of such a fate sent chills up my spine.

I would make sure I ate every last scrap of food on my plate. This was no time to waste. I remembered what my old aunt had said many times about "waste not, want not." Surely, if I ate everything without complaint, God would see to it that we would have enough food to last us over the winter.

The miracle of it all, to me, was that there was always a supper on the table when I came home at night. There was also always a breakfast the next morning and a brown paper bag of lunch to take to the Northcote school. I would go to bed, somewhat content that we had been spared for yet another day.

It finally occurred to me that I was the only one doing the worrying. Mother certainly greeted each day with her usual cheerful manner. If she was worrying about our next meal, she certainly didn't show it.

It was not until years later that I realized the possibility of our starving was very remote indeed. Mother had ways of stretching out the winter stores so that we had plenty to eat. We had enormous pots of soup made from every last onion heel and carrot, leftover roasts and gravies and diced potatoes, which we never seemed to run out of. Johnnycake with home-made brown sugar sauce appeared often when the preserve shelf started to look sparse. The hens seemed to deliver a never-ending supply of fresh eggs, and when the porridge bag was low we had scrambled eggs for breakfast, egg-salad sandwiches for our school lunches and baked custards for supper. When the pork barrel and the smokehouse started to look empty, we had chicken and dumplings, chicken stew and roasted chicken several times a week. Homemade bread and hand-churned butter filled our stomachs, and bread pudding, which has never been one of my favourite desserts, appeared more and more frequently on our supper table.

If we ran out of cocoa, a spoonful of molasses was stirred into our milk as a treat. Custard pies with the crusts made from hand-rendered lard were devoured with gusto. Potatoes went farther if they were cooked with their skins on, and a shank of ham was sliced cold for one meal, diced with a few vegetables and a creamed sauce for another, and finally cut up fine in Mother's wonderful homemade pea soup.

Before I knew it, the back of winter would be broken. Soon there would be big kettles of sap boiling on the Findlay Oval, and Mother would be poring over the seed catalogues deciding what to order for our garden. I would once again be content. The winter would soon be behind us and we would survive—just as we did every year.

Rituals

Mother always said that rituals were good for the soul, the heart and the mind. Rituals, in fact, were more like traditions back in the thirties. They were as much a part of our lives as long underwear and crab-apple jelly.

Our lives were steeped in traditions and so we celebrated every holiday known to man, which didn't always sit well with Father, who even thought Christmas was overdone. Mother honoured every one from Robbie Burns to St. Patrick's. She thought traditions and rituals strengthened the family. Mother had ingenious ways of decorating the house on those special days, coming up with centrepieces for the kitchen table, and embellishments to enhance the old log house. Putting aside all Father's complaints about the nonsense of it all, as a little girl I thought any celebration of anyone's memory or birthday was just fine with me.

I can remember grace at mealtimes. We joined hands to say our thanks for what was before us. I sat beside Father, and I can remember his rough hand over mine, and how without fail, with the last "Amen," I waited for the hard squeeze that always came. Father didn't consider grace frivolous. Not like green cupcakes on St. Patrick's Day, or a piece of plaid gingham over the old pine table on Robbie Burns' birthday, for instance. No, grace was necessary and, in Father's eyes, could hardly be called a tradition.

Another ritual I remember with fondness was how Mother would let each of us choose the supper menu once a week. I always asked for baked beans, because Mother made what she called Boston baked beans, full of salt pork, brown sugar and molasses. Emerson, when it came his turn to choose, always wanted sausages from the smokehouse, homemade apple-sauce and raisin pie, and so the ritual went.

Even though there wasn't much in them, we were always treated to hidden baskets of hard-boiled eggs on Easter morning. The baskets could be found anywhere from the henhouse to the hayloft.

The Christmas tree decorations were scant, but what we had we made ourselves around the kitchen table on what Mother called "our Christmas tree ornament night." I once made a felt donkey when I was about seven; it hung on the tree long after I had grown up.

A tradition I remember with nostalgia was when Mother would sense that all was not well in our world. She said everyone was entitled to a "bad day." When she sensed that one of us was having a bad day, she would do something very special for us. In the summertime it might be nothing more than a special snack on the banks of the Bonnechere River, just her and the one who was sad; in the winter, it might be a trip through the old memory trunk at the top of the stairs. When it was my turn to have a bad day, Mother would spend precious time with me. And on those mornings I was always given a special treat at breakfast— Mother doused fresh homemade bread with lots of butter, put the bread on a tin pie plate and popped it into the Findlay Oval oven where it would crisp up to a golden brown. It was the most delicious way to eat homemade bread, and to this day it's still a special treat for me.

Mother was right when she said rituals and traditions are the stuff of which memories are made. She thought they should be as much a part of our lives as singing and dancing and reading a book from the Renfrew Library. At the time, back in those Depression years, I had a hard time figuring out how traditions and rituals could be good for the heart, soul and mind. But now I know.

Airing Out the House

Mother was what Father called "obsessed" with fresh air. In the summertime this wasn't a problem, but when the freezing blasts of winter settled in around our old log house in Renfrew County, fresh air brought inside was another matter. Father said the whole idea was right up there with using cloth serviettes at the supper table, which was another idea Mother had brought with her from New York, and which he said served no useful purpose whatsoever.

As far as I was concerned there was enough fresh air entering the house without encouraging it further. There was always a draft around the windows, and as much as Mother tried to stop it by forcing old wool socks in around the frames, and laying rolled towels on the sills, you could still feel the blast of winter if you sat close to a window.

During the cold months, our upstairs was like an ice house. Frost formed on the rafters, and sometimes on a blustery day we could find little mounds of snow on the floor under the windows. Yet Mother, every once in a while, felt the need to air out the house.

The only concession Father was able to get from Mother regarding this foolish habit, was that she gave lots of notice when the day came for the event. Usually at breakfast, and only if the sun was shining, Mother would sniff the air in the kitchen, walk over to the parlour door and do the same thing, and announce that it was time the house had a good airing. Father would give a big sigh, and the rest of us would shiver in anticipation. Thankfully, the chore was always done when we were away at school.

That morning Father wouldn't stoke the fire before he went off to the barns to finish up the chores. He would let it die down to embers..."no need to waste good wood heating all of Renfrew County" was his usual comment.

As we five children dressed in our heavy winter clothes, piling layer on top of layer to head out for the three-and-a-half mile walk to the Northcote School, Mother would already be planning her ritual of airing out the house. Opening the packed windows was impossible. It would mean pulling out all the stuffings and using a hot kettle of water to thaw out the ice that locked the windows tight until the spring thaw.

Upstairs in the back bedroom shared by my three brothers, there was a small door sitting right in the middle of one of the walls. No one could figure out why it was there, because it led nowhere. There wasn't so much as a ledge outside the house to stand on. The door served no purpose as far as we could see, but to Mother it was put there for the sole purpose of airing out the house in the dead of winter. Father said that was just more nonsense. He had been born in that house, and until Mother came to make Renfrew County her home, he had never heard of opening the doors wide to the freezing cold to air out the house!

Mother wasted no time getting down to the job at hand. We wouldn't have our hands on the doorknob, before Mother would be heading upstairs to wrench open the small door. By the time we hit the gate at the end of the yard, the kitchen door would be wide open too. Mother would be wrapped in a heavy sweater, and we never knew what she did while the temperature in the house was going down to below zero. Just seeing her standing there waving to us as we headed out the lane sent shivers down my back.

Audrey said she wouldn't be one bit surprised if Mother went through the house waving bedsheets in the doorways to get the stale air out and the fresh air in. The ritual was the same in the summertime except it was to rid the house of the incessant flies that were the bane of her existence.

We knew for a fact that she would have pulled down the feather tickings which covered us in our beds so that everything could be aired out there too. The only positive thing about that exercise was that it was the one morning when we weren't expected to make up our beds.

We were never sure how long she would leave the doors open to the cold blasts of winter, but Father always said it was long enough to put a real chill on the house. He further lamented that it took a good half day to bring the place up to a decent heat again. By the time we got home from school, the entire chore would be done and finished with for another spell.

Mother was always in a wonderful mood after a day of airing out the house. She would go around sniffing the air, as if it had been sprayed with perfume. She said everything smelled as fresh as a daisy. Father said he couldn't smell a bit of difference, especially since he had relit the fire and the house was once again filled with the smell of burning wood and the bit of smoke that always escaped when the stove had to be started from scratch. Nonetheless, Mother insisted the house smelled better.

Audrey and I always insisted our beds were colder than ever the night of the big airing out. And that was because it would take hours for the heat of the Findlay Oval and the pipe that snaked through the upstairs hall to penetrate our thoroughly chilled beds. Mother argued that it was just our imagination.

Airing the house out in the dead of winter was something Mother and Father never did get to agree on all the time we lived on the farm in Renfrew Country. Like so many of Mother's ideas, which Father said would have been better left on the streets of New York City as far as he was concerned, once she made up her mind, there was little anyone could do to change it. As Father said one time, "Your Mother is like our old horse King. When they make up their mind to do something or go somewhere, you're better to roll with the punches. Both of them have a bit of the mule in them."

A New Roof for the Barn

I remember that winter in the thirties as being particularly harsh. We had more rain than snow, which didn't please my brothers, my sister and me one bit. It rained and blew and froze, and day after day we sloshed to school on the Northcote Side Road and often arrived drenched to the skin after our three-and-a-half-mile walk. We would much rather have had lots of snow so that we could slide down the west hill on the cardboard boxes we used as makeshift toboggans, or make snowballs and build our snowman in the backyard.

There was one day I remember above all others. All night long the wind had howled and the rain had pelted the windowpanes in our upstairs bedrooms, keeping my sister Audrey and me awake most of the night. Father kept getting up to check the fire. He was trying to keep the house warm, and yet he had to be careful that he didn't create a flue fire while doing so. Often he said that if our old log house ever ignited, it would go up like a tinderbox, the very thought of which scared the living daylights out of me.

By the time we got out of bed the next morning, the wind was worse and the rain was slashing down against the house like sheets of steel. It was still dark when I heard Father dipper water into the kettle and scrape it across the Findlay Oval. Soon Mother joined him in the kitchen and then, one by one, we children came down the stairs. "Awful storm" was Father's greeting. Daylight was starting to creep into the windows and Father said he was going to make a dash for the barn. He was gone less than a minute when he rushed back into the house, his clothes slick with freezing rain. "Most of the barn roof is gone," he said. Mother just stood there with an disbelieving look on her face. Father said it would have to be fixed immediately or we would lose our hay and grain. "No school today," he added. He said he was taking the team and wagon over to the neighbours' to see if he could borrow some tarpaper until he got into Renfrew and that he would expect us to be ready for work by the time he got back.

Mother made sure we were dressed warmly beneath our heavy outer clothes. There was only one raincoat, which had come in a hand-me-down box from Aunt Lizzie, and Emerson was the only one it fit, so he got it. We left the warmth of the kitchen and put our heads down to plunge into the beating rain. When we reached the barn, Father was just coming into the yard. The wagon was loaded and covered with a big tarpaulin.

In no time the boys had the rolls of tarpaper in the barn, and Father had the ladder leaning against the beam. Audrey and I were to hand up nails and hammers and a sharp knife to cut the paper. Mother was right up in the rafters with the boys and Father. They worked feverishly against the pounding rain, which showed no sign of letting up. I could see Mother's black hair plastered against her face, and ice was forming on Father's overalls. The boys said their arms ached from carrying the rolls up the ladder, but still we worked on. Often it looked like the weather was going to win the battle. The wind had taken off most of the roof. Father told Audrey and I to get up in the haymow and cover as much as we could with the horse blankets. My stomach told me it must be din-nertime, but there was no mention of stopping to eat.

Father had nailed boards from beam to beam to hold the tarpaper and said it would only be a temporary measure until the roof could be fixed properly. His main worry was saving what grain and hay we had to see us through the long winter ahead. It was late day when Father drove in the last nail.

We were exhausted when Father, Mother and the boys climbed down the ladders. We stood back and surveyed the repair job. Father said it looked pretty good to him. We were soaked to the skin again as we trudged through the howling wind and rain back to the house.

Even though it was still daylight, Mother sent us up to get into our clean, warm, flannelette pyjamas. When we came down, she and Father were in dry clothes and the old Findlay Oval was jumping. Father was frying sauerkraut and Mother was heating milk for hot chocolate. Audrey cut a loaf of homemade bread into big chunks, and I was sent to the cupboard for a jar of preserves. Everett was putting back bacon in the big iron frypan, and Emerson uttered not a sound of complaint when Mother asked him to set the table.

Soon it became dark, and the coal-oil lamp was lit. The kitchen became a haven from the raging rain and wind outside. When we finally sat down for our first meal of the day, Father said a long and purposeful grace. He looked at each of us in turn and said, "We could go into the roofing business, we could." And I knew what he meant then when he said that teamwork would get us through those Depression years. I felt the utmost contentment as I looked around the table.

When Dirt is a Dirty Word

As far as Mother was concerned, dirt was dirt, plain and simple. Father on the other hand, thought that sometimes dirt was not only completely acceptable, it was a mark of distinction. It took me a long time to learn what that word meant. Father explained it this way.

He used as an example our neighbour who had just moved to Renfrew County from the city. He was called a "gentleman farmer." Father said the only difference between this newcomer and the rest of the farmers on the Northcote Side Road was that the local farmers got their living from the land, while this man got his living from his stocks and bonds in the city. Father said he knew this for a fact, because he never saw the man with dirty hands.

After hearing this, I took to looking at the man's hands every time I saw him. Father was absolutely right. While Father's hands were gnarled and rough from hard work, and always covered with grass stains, with fingernails that were never quite rid of black grease from patching up the ancient machinery, this newcomer's hands were as white as lilies. Father said he suspected his wife even polished his nails.

Mother said he wore the marks of a gentleman, a statement that sent Father into a long tirade about an honest day's work. Father always maintained that any farmer who landed at Briscoe's General Store in the middle of the day with clean overalls hadn't much to show for spending a day at farm chores. Even though Mother would beg him to change his clothes before he went off on a farm errand, Father would flatly refuse. He almost never contradicted Mother, but on this issue he held his ground.

Father would change his clothes only if he was going into Renfrew to sit on the main street on a Saturday night. On a weekday, the old overalls with the dirt from the land and barns and livestock, were worn like a badge of honour. Clean dirt, he would call it.

Mother said she could never understand how a man who refused to wear clean overalls could keep such a tidy barn. The barns were cleaned out sometimes twice a day and always done to his liking too! On more than one occasion, we had to do the job over again if we missed a bit of manure in a gutter. He couldn't abide his animals standing in a barnyard full of mud. In the spring, or in the rainy season, he kept moving the cows and the pigs to a dry spot, rather than have them knee-deep in dirt.

Clean overalls were an entirely different matter. Father did abide by Mother's wishes, though, and hung them in the summer kitchen before he came into the house for a meal, arriving in the kitchen in his long underwear. He knew full well when he stripped himself of the overalls on Sunday night, he wouldn't see them on the nail in the summer kitchen the next morning. Handling them like they were sprayed with some sort of poison, Mother would drop the overalls beside the kitchen stove, ready for the washtub on Monday morning, lamenting all the while that it would take a miracle to get the dirt out. Father was forced to put on the clean pair that Mother had placed on the same nail for the next morning. He often said it took him the better part of the week just to break in the clean overalls.

When an election rolled around and one of the local farmers was running for office, Father said he would never vote for a man who came to the house who was ashamed to wear his work clothes, dirt and all. Mother said she never heard of such nonsense.

I can't say Mother and Father ever fought over the issue, but as long as we lived on the farm, Father believed the mark of a good farmer was how well his overalls had been "worked in," as he called it. How different they were. Mother would cover a soiled housedress with a clean white pinny if she heard a car drive into the yard, while Father would stride out from the barns, rub his stained hands down the side of his well-dirtied overalls, and greet whoever it was as if he was wearing his Sunday suit.

Often I would wonder at this mild conflict in our household over dirt and I would ask Father about it. He would say, "You can't work and have clean hands. And that's a fact. And when you are a farmer, you get to know the difference between clean and dirty dirt."

A Privilege and a Duty

Mother believed it was not only a privilege to go to the polls to vote, but a duty. Father, on the other hand, felt his duty ended when he didn't like the candidate who was running for reeve. He simply stayed home and refused to cast a ballot.

When election time rolled around, we children could count on a battle royal between Mother and Father. They not only disagreed on the obligation of casting one's vote, but always, as long as I can remember, disagreed on the candidates as well. Father tended to favour the old tried and true, while Mother's favourite comment was "a new broom sweeps clean." It was years before I was able to figure that one out.

One election I remember in particular was the year Father decided he wasn't going to the polls. His favourite candidate, who had been reeve for many years, had decided not to run. This decision Father likened to a national calamity. Father said the two young whippersnappers who were trying for the township's top office could never replace the old veteran.

Father also knew that one of the candidates had a grandfather who was caught sheep stealing, and he wouldn't be a bit surprised if the trait hadn't filtered down to the grandson. Mother said the idea was sheer nonsense, and didn't Father know that the young man in question attended the United Church regularly? That was all Father needed to hear. He never did trust a United Church adherent, and said the only honourable people he knew in Renfrew County were Lutherans! As far as the other candidate was concerned, he was one of those newfangled farmers who came out from the city with the idea of turning the whole county around to his liking. He couldn't be trusted either. No, he wasn't going to vote, and that was the simple truth of the matter. Mother said he was a stubborn old German, and she didn't care if he voted or not, but he certainly wasn't going to keep her away from the polls.

That year the day of the election rolled around crisp and cold. Father made it known at the breakfast table that he had absolutely no intention of changing his mind about voting, and he would be much obliged if no one mentioned going to the polls to him for the rest of the day!

Mother announced to anyone who cared to take heed that it didn't matter a whit to her if he went or stayed home. It was a privilege and a duty to vote. She'd be going later in the day and was to take old Granny Hines from the next farm as well. She had talked Granny into voting for the candidate of her choice and promised to take the old woman after she had her afternoon nap. Father grunted his disapproval and headed for the barns. The school was used as a polling station, so we five children had a holiday, which was the main reason I got excited about elections back in the thirties.

Just an hour before the polls closed, Mother headed for the drive shed to back out the Model T. We could see Father's image in the cow byre window. Mother was all dressed up for the occasion. She ordered Everett to man the crank and she settled herself behind the wheel. Everett cranked and cranked and nothing happened. He came around to the driver's side and told Mother to pull down on the gas lever. He tried again. There wasn't a sign of life in the old Model T. Mother thought it may have been flooded, and she said to let it rest for a while. I could see smoke from Father's pipe coming out the cow byre door, but he made no move to help Mother.

I was sent to the kitchen to get the right time. Now there was less than half an hour to pick up Granny Hines and drive to Northcote. Hitching up the buggy would do no good; there wasn't time. Finally, Mother got out and manned the crank. The old car didn't even murmur. She sent

Audrey scurrying over to Granny Hines' to tell her the trip to the polls was off. Mother climbed out of the car and slowly headed for the house.

The polls would be closed in minutes. It was then Father came from the barn, walked into the drive shed and pulled a feed bag off a rain barrel in the corner. There was the battery from the Model T! Father said he was getting ready to put the car away for the winter, and that day seemed as good a day as any to make a start.

It is no exaggeration to say Mother was furious. She had not only missed her vote, but the way she told it, the future of Renfrew County could easily rise or fall on that missed vote alone.

I remember other elections while we lived on the farm. All of them were filled with excitement and they almost always created a confrontation between Mother and Father. As soon as the polls closed, however, all was forgotten. There were more pressing concerns of the thirties to be dealt with.

Yard Day

Every year when winter gave way to spring, Mother and Father would engage in what we children called "working towards opposite ends to arrive at the same destination." At the time it took me a while to figure out exactly what my sister Audrey was talking about. She explained it to me with great patience, and I, too, soon mastered the phrase and was able to turn it at the drop of a hat.

Mother thought that cleaning up the yard in the spring was just as important as doing the annual housecleaning. And she likened that chore to going to church every Sunday.

Father, on the other hand, was quite content to let the spring winds and rain take care of last fall's leaves. About all that he was willing to contribute was a kick with the toe of his boot if there were any broken branches lying on the front lawn.

The funny thing was that they both liked to have nice flowers. They each had a great fondness for flowers of every description, although they had their own personal favourites. While Mother liked a neat front yard, Father was far more interested in a flower bed.

Father could work his flower beds, digging the soil and turning it with the blunt-nosed shovel until it was as fine as sand. He'd work in fertilizer, which he hauled from the back of the barn in the wheelbarrow. Every stray blade of grass was hand-picked in preparation of where to plant the little packets of seeds he had bought from Scott's Hardware.

He would draw big circles with a stick and, muttering to himself, he'd declare which part of the flower bed was for asters and which for snap-dragons, his two favourites. Hours were spent down on his hands and knees, until he had every inch of the flower gardens plotted out the way he fancied.

If Mother asked him to so much as remove a fallen branch from the yard, he'd say there was no need. That was what a yard was for! Only if it prevented him from driving the old Model T over the spot where it hit the ground, should it be moved.

This is where Mother and Father differed greatly. Mother liked the flower beds, but she never had much patience with the planting. If they came up, well and good, but if they didn't, that was quite all right too. She was much more interested in having the front and side yards immaculate.

Every year at springtime, when it was apparent that she wasn't going to have much luck at pressing Father into service, Mother would announce on a Saturday morning that this was "yard day." Emerson, Earl and Everett would groan, and Audrey and I would resign ourselves to the fact that we would be spending the entire day out in our yard. That also meant that our usual Saturday visits with school friends would be suspended.

We children would put on the oldest overalls we could find, along with our rubber boots, because often the yard had yet to dry up. Audrey and I tied big red bandanas around our heads, and as soon as the kitchen was redded up in the morning, we'd head for the yard.

We raked from one end to the other, which was no easy feat as our yard was enormous. In a few minutes, I would have a big blister between my thumb and forefinger. I can remember as if it were yesterday, how my shoulders would ache. To ask to go into the house was to invite a long lecture from Mother on everyone working together, and hearing for the millionth time that "many hands make light work." Emerson could be heard muttering, "if my hands last that long."

By this time, of course, Father would have vanished. He thought the whole idea of cleaning up a farmyard was sheer nonsense. Let them carry on that silliness in the town of Renfrew, he'd lament, but he was having no part of it out there in Northcote. He pretended not hear when

Mother reminded him of the time and effort he put into his flower beds.

When we thought we had every stray leaf gathered and stuffed into the barrel for burning, Mother would scan the yard to make sure we hadn't missed anything. If it met with her satisfaction, she would bring out the can of paint and we'd take turns painting the iron pump and platform that sat in the middle of the yard. Of course, while we were at it, we might as well do the big wire gates. I thought there was nothing in the world more hateful than painting wire gates!

By suppertime the yard would be full of the smells of burning debris. Father would have long since finished his flower beds. We'd stumble into the house, incoherent from exhaustion.

As he did every year, Father would feel a moment of remorse for not having pitched in, and he'd offer to make supper that night. That ritual never varied all the time we lived on the farm in Renfrew County. Mother would sigh in gratitude as we all headed for the wash basin and the huck towel. We'd strip to our underwear, piling our muddy and smoke-drenched clothes in the summer kitchen for the Monday wash.

Father always served us a big, rib-sticking German meal. He's cut up a slab of salt pork, fill a pan with buttered sauerkraut, open a jar of dill pickles and whip up a batch of his famous German potato pancakes. We all ate like it was our last meal on earth, and the toil of the day would almost be forgotten. Of course, the blisters on our hands and the smokey smell of burning leaves, which hung inside the house like incense, would be reminders of our accomplishments for days to come.

Away from Home

What a wonderful experience it was going to be for me! My very first overnight trip, all by myself, away from my Northcote home. Oh, I had been to Montreal and to Ottawa, but always I was with the rest of the family. And certainly I had slept many times overnight at my little friend Velma's house. That never really felt like being away from home, because when Velma and I were ready to crawl between the big feather tickings, I would scoot over to the south window and look across the fields. I could see the coal-oil light shining from my own kitchen window. Mother always put the lamp in the window when I went to Velma's, just so I could see it before I went to bed. I always felt if there was a real emergency, I could always scoot home. The only emergency, of course, would be that I would be stricken with a severe case of homesickness.

Now, I was going all the way to Arnprior to stay overnight at my Aunt Nellie's and Uncle Henry's house. I was so excited, I didn't know how I was going to stand it. My father was to drive me over on Saturday morning, and as early as Wednesday I had packed and unpacked the little cardboard suitcase a dozen times.

Aunt Nellie's house was so special. We had visited many times, and in it were all the things I thought were reserved for the very wealthy. Uncle Henry worked at the Kenwood Woollen Mill, and we thought he must at least be president, because the house he and Aunt Nellie lived in was red brick, with a wide verandah painted battleship grey. On the verandah were big wooden lounge chairs in kelly green. Uncle Henry wore a suit to work with a white shirt and tie. Wasn't that proof enough that he was either president or part owner of the mill?

To me, the inside of the house was just as impressive as the outside. In the kitchen was a big white porcelain sink, and a gadget which Aunt Nellie could get to spew out water by simply turning on an iron tap. I was sure she would encourage me to have a bath in the elegant bathtub which sat high on brass legs and had claw feet. I had never had a bath before in anything other than our big oval copper tub, sitting close to the Findlay Oval in the kitchen on a Saturday night. My whole body was tingling with excitement just thinking about what was in store for me. By far, though, the very best part of Aunt Nellie's house was what she called the guest room. I knew it would be all mine for that very first night away from home.

The whole room was decorated in apple green, and even the spindle bed had been painted the softest green to match the organza curtains and the crocheted bedspread. The mattress sat high, and a little footstool, also painted apple green, sat beside the bed. When Aunt Nellie took me upstairs, she placed my suitcase on it so it would be easy to reach.

It soon came time for Father to leave, and I felt a moment of sheer panic when I realized I was on my own. Aunt Nellie must have anticipated what was going through my mind, because her arm fell lightly on my shoulders as we waved goodbye, and at once, I felt warm and secure.

Alas, the feeling was short-lived. Night soon closed in on the town of Arnprior and the lovely red brick house. Too soon I found myself being tucked into the green spindle bed, and then Aunt Nellie turned the light out and was gone. I lay in the bed as stiff as a board. Even though it was summer I was overcome with shivers and shakes and was freezing from fright. The whole room was so bright, it was like daylight, with the streetlight shining right in the window. I could hear Uncle Henry listening to the radio in the parlour below, and the cars that went up and down the street. I found the town noises deafening. Out on the farm in Northcote, when the last lamp was blown out, there wasn't a sound to be heard other than the gentle sounds of a country night. That peacefulness lulled me to sleep and gave me the feeling of utmost peace and safety. I had no idea how I was going to put in a whole night of noise and confusion in Arnprior.

What seemed like hours dragged by, and the situation did not improve. I longed for the gentle sound of a whippoorwill or a frog or my mother moving quietly around the kitchen below. Most of all I longed for the darkness which enveloped the entire farm when night came. I wanted the security of my Northcote farm. I found that I hated the silky bedsheets, and I pined for the feeling of the flour-bag linen. Nothing creaked in this house of Aunt Nellie's! It stood solid and silent like a stranger. On top of it all, I was so lonesome for Mother, that I couldn't imagine how I was going to survive the night with touching her face or smelling her hair.

Sleep eventually overcame me, and when I opened my eyes the sunlight was pouring in the little casement windows. The green room was once again like something I would find in a picture book from the Renfrew Library. My concerns in the dark Arnprior night vanished with the daylight.

Thinking back now, that night taught me an important lesson. To live on a farm in the Ottawa Valley meant that there were more important things than brick houses, water that came out of a tap, and lights that turned on with a switch. What really mattered was being part of the big warm family, and being surrounded by all that was dear and familiar. Although I never lost the awe I felt when I visited Aunt Nellie in her magnificent brick home, I knew, too, that there was really nothing wrong with the old log house out at Northcote either.

The Unexpected Guest

The kitchen table was always set for dinner before we went to bed on Christmas Eve. The big pine table that sat against the west wall was stretched out as far as it would go. Days before Christmas, Mother would have taken the long, white linen cloth out of the trunk in the upstairs hall, and it would be washed, starched and ironed. This task took hours of her time, but as this was the most important meal of the entire year, everything had to be just perfect.

Although we didn't own a complete set of dishes, an effort was made to put out the very best we had. This meant matching up all those pieces we had collected from either Theatre Night in Renfrew or from the big bags of puffed wheat from Briscoe's General Store. Mother would put her best geranium in the centre of the table, and circle it with pieces of green cedar. The red broadcloth napkins, which were only used at that time of the year, were also used in the setting of the table

It was my sister Audrey's and my task to set the table before we got ready for bed on Christmas Eve. Without fail, Father, who never took an interest at any other time, would hover over the table as if he alone was in charge of the Christmas dinner. He would instruct us to be sure to set an extra place at the end of the table. And then, as he did every year, he told us about the German custom his family had carried on as long as he could remember. They always set an extra place at the end of the table for an unexpected guest. Father would say that we were blessed with an ample table, and if anyone came hungry, we could assure the visitor of a full plate. I always asked him if the guest ever showed up. Father would look very mysterious indeed, and say that we would never know for sure because sometimes the unexpected guest could not be seen.

That would send shivers right up my spine. Mother had little patience with Father's German folklore, but she indulged him at Christmastime, and by the time we went to bed, there would be the place at the head of the table for the unexpected guest.

One Christmas, when we came home from church, we could see from the end of the lane that someone was standing at our back door. As the sleigh got closer to the house we could see an old battered tapestry bag at her feet. Only when we rounded the corner at the summer kitchen did we recognize Father's old aunt. She was the one who came every fall to mend socks, knit mitts and sew buttons on our winter shirts, before going off to another relative's farm to help at sap time. We hardly ever saw her except during those few weeks late in the fall, but here she was, standing on our back stoop.

She was ushered in and welcomed like the much-loved aunt she was. The smells of the turkey cooking in the Findlay Oval met us when we opened the door, and the warmth of the kitchen was like a friendly arm reaching around us. When it came time to sit down at the ample Christmas table, Auntie was given the extra place at the end of the table which Audrey and I had set the night before.

As we all settled into our places, Father passed the back of my chair and ran his hand over my hair. In the softest voice, close to my ear, he said, "Sometimes the unexpected guest is someone we know."

Family

I don't suppose our family is that much different from any other. We have had our ups and downs, and have managed to survive the best and the worst of times. When I look around me, I have a lot for which to be grateful. We enjoy the niceties of life and a good standard of living in this abundant land.

When I say my prayers and give my thanks for the many blessings that come into my life every day, I often wonder if our station in life has a lot to do with being in the right place at the right time, or if, in fact, it has more to do with perseverance and an upbringing that settled for nothing less than performing to the best of our abilities.

At an early age it was drilled into us that our capabilities were unlimited and we could do just about anything we wanted to do if we wanted to do it badly enough. Often my older sister Audrey pondered her future and gently questioned our parents' philosophy. She would contemplate what lay ahead for her and wondered if it was indeed possible to reach for the stars when your beginnings were of the humblest kind—growing up in a small log house in a remote part of the country, with few amenities, and with never enough money to enjoy even the most basic of comforts. You see, it was the Depression. But nonetheless, our parents drummed into her that going beyond the circumstances which surrounded us would be entirely up to her.

As I grew older, the same message was given to me. I realized that what I did with my life and what I made of it would be my responsibility, and my destiny would be in my own hands.

From an early age, I learned that family was of the utmost importance. We grew up with regular visits from relatives from every part of the country. Often our little house with its kitchen, parlour, small bedroom downstairs and three equally small rooms upstairs would be bursting at the seams. It seems to me now, it was a rare week indeed when our family was alone. Aunts came from the West, cousins from the United States, relatives from the city. They all came to "get a breath of good clean country air," as my Grandfather called it. Some, my father said, came to get fed. They would leave with their cars packed with freshly plucked chickens, a bag of new potatoes, big brown eggs, and roasts from the smokehouse. I thought these city relatives would be very rich indeed. But they weren't. We were the ones that were rich, with an abundant root cellar full of vegetables, and a full pork and sauerkraut barrel in the summer kitchen. Many came while passing by on a trip leading elsewhere. But some came and stayed. And stayed.

Take the old woman who I always thought was an aunt, but many years later I learned she wasn't. She was related, but the connection was so remote that no one ever stopped to figure it all out.

She would arrive before Christmas with all her earthly possessions tucked into a small tapestry bag. She came supposedly to knit new mitts, sew lugs on toques, darn socks and patch worn-out overalls. By spring she would pack up and go off to another 'relative,' because it was sap time, and she was needed. We would hear that by midsummer she had gone on to another farm because it was threshing time, and there were meals to help prepare for the gangs of neighbours who congregated to help with the harvest. By October, she would have wended her way to another 'kin' to help the men bring logs out of the bush.

It was many years later that I learned she had no home. She survived by going from home to home and doing what she called "earning her keep." The alternative to living and working with her relatives would be the County Home. The poorhouse.

Auntie's situation was not unusual in those times. Today, there are modern and well-run nursing and seniors' homes and retirement centres. But until the advent of these options, the only choice was living with whoever would take you in. And when my sister Audrey and I complained when we had to give up our bed and sleep on the creton couch in the kitchen, Mother called it "character building."

Character building indeed! Time would prove that I would need it. It wasn't long after I was married that my husband's father came to live with us. He was aged. Very aged, I thought as a young bride. Wally was an only child and his mother had died before we were married. There was no thought of putting Grampa into a nursing home. Born in Scotland, he was in his seventies and badly crippled with arthritis. He settled right in and stayed seventeen years. Before he died in his late eighties, my mother lost a leg and came to live with us too. That put four generations under our roof. Grampa in his eighties, Mother in her early seventies, Wally and I, and three young children.

It was the happiest of times and it was the toughest of times. Our children learned, too, about character building, just as I did when I had to relinquish a bed when I was seven years old. The rewards far outweighed the costs. Our children learned about barrel staving in Scotland, and what it was like to roam the Highlands and ride a ship on the North Sea. Our little girls learned to make gingerbread cookies, ice a cake, and whip up pancakes. And we all learned to sacrifice. We all learned that the right way isn't always the easiest.

Many of the lessons I learned as a young child growing up on the farm during those Depression years are with me to this day. I learned that as a parent you have a grave responsibility to lead your children into adulthood along a path that will help them make the right decisions. You try to tell them that their choices will affect them the rest of their lives.

Sometimes you will fail, and you will feel guilty, but I have learned that not only is it part of the parenting process to fail on occasion, it is perfectly normal to feel guilty when you do.

I also learned that I have a responsibility to myself. If I am to reach my fulfillment as an aging parent and grandparent, I have to live by the words of the Serenity Prayer: "God grant me serenity to accept the things I cannot change, courage to change the things I can, and wisdom to know the difference."

We are inextricably linked to our pasts. If family was the dominant force in our lives when we were children, if we were raised with the belief that a loving family is paramount, then that is the belief we live with in the present.

The next section in this book is all about family. Here are the people and stories that have shaped my life. What I am, or am not, today is directly bonded to those who formed my family from the day of my birth to the present. These, then, are their stories.

Anticipating the Long Nights Ahead

Just like the squirrels I watched out in the yard, as they hoarded food for the onslaught of winter, we children, too, anticipated the long hours when we sat huddled around the kitchen table close to the cookstove.

To get ready for what we knew would be many evenings with little in the way of entertainment, every fall we went out to what we called the 'gravel-pit bush.' We were equipped with sharp jackknives, and because I was the youngest, I was given the job of carrying the flat cardboard box saved year after year just for that purpose.

In this small cluster of trees was a stand of birch. Glistening white, the trees stood out like a beacon when the sun shone, and I wonder now that they survived at all after what we did to them every year.

The boys, using the sharp knives, would ever so carefully cut off pieces of birch bark, being especially careful to keep each portion intact. They got quite expert at it. First, they would mark out the square with the knife, and then very carefully peel it back, being sure not to cut too deeply. Then they would slide the blade under the cut, and ever so carefully lift out the piece of birch bark. It was my job to follow the brothers like a servant, and they would very carefully set the piece of bark into the box I was carrying. Sometimes my brother Everett would let me lift off a piece of the bark, but I soon learned that peeling was a real art, and that I had a long way to go before I could skin the bark from the tree while keeping it in one piece.

Usually we would have to make several trips back to the gravel-pit bush. We had to be sure we had enough birch bark to last us for the winter. When we got it back to the house, the box was stored in the summer kitchen for a few days to let the bark rest, as Father called it. I would check it often. I have no idea why. Perhaps I thought someone would run off with it when I wasn't looking.

The bark became part of our winter's entertainment. We had other things to do to occupy our time on an evening when the wind and the snow pounded against the old log house, but I don't think anything gave us more pleasure than those pieces of birch bark. When we knew we were going to be using them that night, before we went off to school in the morning we would either soak them in a pan of water, or we would put them between two pieces of old towelling Mother kept for us for just that purpose. That evening when we had redded up the kitchen and when the house had settled down, we would take the damp pieces of bark to the kitchen table and each of us with our own portions would go to work.

The boys usually made small canoes which were only about six inches long. They would cut and shape and stick the pieces together with home-made paste. To make sure they would hold, they would clip them with Mother's clothespins. Many of their creations tested the imagination, and it was sometimes difficult to determine just exactly what the boys had made. Many a time I thought the last thing the creation looked like was a canoe; to my brothers, however, they were as fine as any turned out by a native Indian.

These little canoes had very few uses, so often by the time the winter was over, they were abandoned. My sister Audrey and I, although I must admit now that it was mostly Audrey, chose to make little square boxes. We cut out the pieces, making sure they all matched perfectly, and using Mother's big darning needle or the awl, we made holes all along the edges. We then took pieces of coloured yarn and blanket-stitched them together forming the box.

I thought our creations were much more useful than silly canoes which really in my mind were good for nothing. Mother used our little boxes for hairpins and buttons, and Audrey and I always made sure there were one or two on the washstand in our bedroom for all the little odds and ends we collected.

In an era when there were no radios, we depended on our own ingenuity to keep ourselves amused. Simple pieces of birch bark gave us many an hour of enjoyment. And, like so many of the blessings of the thirties, the price tag was exactly right.

Grass

Very few of our farm neighbours paid much attention to the grass in the front yards. Some had those old-fashioned push mowers with figure-eight blades, but most of us waited until the grass was calf high and then someone took a scythe to it and brought it down to ankle level.

One neighbour kept a couple of goats, and Father said they did a much better job on the grass than any newfangled lawnmower. Mother wouldn't hear of goats roaming the front yard. She was positive they would eat the laundry lying on the grass to dry, slurp up her precious rainwater, and make short work of her flower garden.

For long spells, the grass in our yard was allowed to grow willy-nilly, which suited my sister Audrey and me just fine. The long grass allowed us to while away a few hours at one of our favourite pastimes. This time of year, when the sun beat down on the old farmhouse, so hot and piercing that it dried and cracked the clay at the back door, Audrey and I would seek a quiet spot under the big elm tree. Here the grass wasn't as high as it was in other parts of the yard, so we would go to a spot near the gate and carefully pull great handfuls of it, mindful that it was very important to keep the blades in one piece. The success of what we were going to do with them depended entirely on their not being broken. And when we had as many blades as Audrey thought we needed, we would head for the coolness of the big tree and fold ourselves down on the ground.

My job was to sort the blades into bundles of three, making sure that they were all the same length. I was so thrilled to be part of something that involved my much older and certainly much wiser sister, that I took meticulous care to do exactly as I was told.

I would have all the grass fanned out on the skirt of my cotton dress, and Audrey would take forever to decide which bundle of three she would pick first. I would be filled with impatience and want to yell out, "Hurry...I can't wait forever," but I knew better than to rush Audrey.

She would make her choice, pointing a finger at a bundle. I would pick it up carefully, and hold the very ends of the three blades between my thumb and forefinger. Then Audrey would lean over and with her long thin fingers she would take the other ends of the three blades and she would braid the grass in flat plaits. I would watch her work and think she was just about the cleverest girl in all of Renfrew County.

It never occurred to me that perhaps there were other teenage girls who could braid grass too. As far as I was concerned, Audrey was the only one on the Northcote Side Road who could do such a clever feat. I would watch her very carefully, knowing that she would soon ask me if I was ready to try it.

The first time I attempted to braid grass, Audrey almost lost patience with me. I was braiding it too tightly, and it broke. I didn't remember to press the braid down with my fingers to make it flat.

Each time I tried after that I would be close to tears, wondering if I would ever be able to perform this most clever task. Just when I was about ready to give up, Audrey would tell me she knew I could do it, and there it would be—a braid of grass not any longer than six inches. I would just about burst with pride as my sister heaped praise on my achievement.

By today's standards, I don't suppose there is anything too remarkable about braiding grass. I doubt that anyone even does it anymore...except me of course. Looking back now, I realize that it wasn't only learning the trick of braiding grass that was so important. It was that wonderful quiet time with a special sister, so much older, who must have had better things to do than sit under a tree with a seven-year-old. Audrey took the time anyway because she knew how I loved it when we did things together.

When I want to recapture, for a fleeting moment, that feeling of closeness we shared so many years ago, I find some long blades of grass from the side of our country road, and I sit under a tree and I braid it into short, flat plaits.

Sap Time

Making maple syrup was a yearly task. Just like bottling pickles, or putting down raspberry preserves, the maple syrup we made each year gave variety to our meals and replaced the sweet treats we were unable to buy. Although we ate very well (it was a poor farmer indeed who could not provide his family with ample supplies of vegetables, fruit and meats), we lacked the special treats more affluent people were able to put on their tables. Treats such as oranges and bananas, store-bought jams and chocolate candies were almost unheard of, so the yearly yield of maple syrup was met with much anticipation.

There were always big preserving pots on the back of the Findlay Oval, simmering down clear white sap until it turned the colour of gold and thickened enough to pour into sterilized bottles that once held vinegar, molasses or ketchup. This syrup was for our own use, and it was usually slurped up with homemade bread long before the next batch was ready.

In the meantime, out in the sugar bush, a big flat tin container sat over smouldering logs. It was filled with sap, too, and had to be tended almost twenty-four hours a day. The responsibility of the boiling vat in the bush was pretty much left to my father and brothers until the year Mother went back, for reasons which I no longer remember, and discovered that the syrup-making process was less than sanitary in her eyes.

Mother and I arrived at the site, after walking through knee-high snow. We saw the big, flat-bottomed vat simmering away with smoke seeping out from every side while Father circled it with a long pole in his hand. At the end of the pole were several layers of screening, just like the kind that filled our windows in the summer time. They were cut into shapes that measured about ten inches square. He used this contraption to scoop off foam that formed from the simmering. Mother also noticed that he used the scoop to lift off bits and pieces of twigs, the odd dead leaf, and anything else that fell into the pan.

Only when the soft wind blew through the trees could we see Father's face clearly amidst the steam from the boiling sap. Mother went closer and peered into the liquid. She watched Father scoop out another load of debris. I knew what was coming.

"What would stop an animal from getting into that, Albert?" she asked with innocence. "Well, he wouldn't last long," Father replied, as he continued to scoop foam and debris from the bubbling mixture.

Mother curled her lip in disgust, and I could already see a plot forming in her mind. She hustled me back on the trail through the bush, mumbling all the way about dead animals and goodness knows what all ending up in our maple syrup. I knew for a fact that she was going to end that nonsense, once and for all!

She went right to the drive shed. This was where everything was stored, including the old Model T that was still up on blocks for the winter. There were kegs of nails, tools, rolled-up cardboard and a long piece of chicken wire, which Mother had zeroed in on as she came through the door.

It was meant to be for a new chicken coop that Father never did get around to making. Mother laid it out on the packed-sand floor and measured it off by striding over it. "Just about perfect," she said, and she rolled it up as tight as possible and tucked it under her arm. She then announced that we were heading back to the sugar bush.

Now she had a purpose, and we covered the mile or so in jig time. Father was still scooping off foam from the boiling sap as Mother told him that she had the perfect solution for keeping dirt out of the pan. Father knew what she was up to, and he made no move to help her as she struggled to unroll the wide chicken wire over the top of the pan. I was ordered to stand on one end, and she stretched the remainder of the wire taut over the top. Realizing she couldn't stand there twenty-four hours a day to hold the wire down, she found pieces of log which were destined for the fire, and thus anchored both ends of the wire over the pan. She dusted off her hands and asked Father if he didn't think that made more sense. "It'll keep everything nice and clean," she said. Father asked her how she figured he'd get in with the scoop to take off the foam. Mother said she was sure he would figure something out. With that she took me by the hand and headed back to the house where preparations for the evening meal were about to get underway.

Mother seemed more than pleased with her invention, and she asked Father when he was washing up for supper how it had worked out. "Just fine," he answered, a little too quickly I thought. Mother wore that I-told-you-so look, and nothing more was said.

The next day I headed back to the bush alone as I often did, to spend the day with Father. He was at his usual post. The long scooper was in his hand, but there was no sign of the chicken wire over the vat. And then I saw it—all rolled up as neat as you please, leaning against a tree with a log holding it in place. Thrown over the top was Father's big red plaid coat. On the very top was his fur-lugged hat, and hanging from a bent nail, hooked onto the double wire was Father's honey pail of lunch. "Everything has a purpose," he grinned. We both knew Mother would never know from me what use the chicken wire was ultimately put to.

Emerson the Genius

Mother saw Emerson through entirely different eyes than did anyone else. We all thought he had invented juvenile delinquency. She thought he was brilliant. Looking back, I know now she had good reason to think her son was as smart, or smarter, than anyone who went to the Northcote School.

Because of her belief in him, she indulged his every whim when it came to his creativity. He always said he wanted to build buildings when he grew up. None of us knew what the word architect meant, but that was what Emerson wanted to be. He said simply, that he wanted to build things. So when money was scarcer than feathers on a pig, Mother would go into Ritza's Drugstore in Renfrew and lay out hard-to-come-by cash for things like art gums, soft pencils and big pads of drawing paper. Audrey and I thought it was sheer nonsense, and such a waste of hard-earned money. If we as much as asked for something as frivolous as a bottle of cologne, we got the usual lecture on the Depression; whereas, Emerson had only to say he was getting low on drawing paper, and Mother would kill a few extra chickens, mould a couple more pounds of homemade butter and head into town.

Audrey and I could make no earthly sense out of the things Emerson drew. He used his new ruler and his soft pencils, erasing only occasionally, and drew the most outlandish buildings we ever saw in our lives.

Some of them had no walls on the inside, just big open spaces. Often the outsides were nothing but sheer glass, with jut-outs…and with glass elevators going up on the outside of the buildings, which we thought was the craziest thing we ever saw. Who ever heard of an elevator on the outside of a building? And imagine whole, big office buildings with no partitions. Nonsense, that's what it was, sheer nonsense. And we'd laugh, and slap our thighs, and tease this brother with the vivid imagination, wondering where our mother ever got the notion that she was dealing with someone of high intelligence. On occasion we were sent to our beds for making fun of Emerson. Here we would continue our giggling, and wonder how long it would take Mother to realize she had a strange one for a son.

Emerson kept all these drawings under his bed with his precious collection of maps. He longed for a desk of his own, so that his work, as he called it, would be there for public scrutiny. The end of the old pine table in the kitchen was the closest he ever got to a desk. He talked constantly about going off to school to learn to draw buildings properly. And Mother went right along with his notions. She thought that was a noble idea indeed.

He often refused to show us what he was drawing, knowing full well we would have a laugh at his silly glass buildings. As soon as he would have a drawing completed to his satisfaction he would pull the sheet off the pad, wrap it in tissue paper, and tuck it under his bed with his precious maps of faraway countries. Mother thought this was another sign of brilliance, and threatened us with instant mutilation if we as much as put a finger on his drawings.

Now, so long after those Depression years, I wonder where those drawings have gone. I look at the glass buildings around the world today, and see elevators going up the outside of them. I have walked through offices with no walls, and my mind reflects back to the thirties, and a brother whose dream it was to one day build the kinds of buildings he envisioned in *his* mind's eye, and which are so much a part of our landscape today.

As long as we lived on the farm in Renfrew County, Emerson filled his spare hours with his drawings...oh, he still had enough time left over to torment my sister Audrey and me and create daydreams that were beyond belief. One such drawing stands out in my mind, even though so many years have come and gone. It was a drawing of a glass privy. Emerson visualized it sitting there near the back summer kitchen, fashioned entirely of see-through glass and drawn to perfect scale.

When we got over our laughing fit, we asked him who would ever in a million years want to use a glass privy. His answer was typical of Emerson. "People from another planet, of course. They are all around us now. We can't see them, but they are here." His eyes became slits, as they always did when he got on one of his scientific, unrealistic, daydreaming kicks. "And one day, we'll go to the moon...and we'll build glass buildings...you wait and see."

"Sure, Emerson," we said to humour him. Sure, we will.

Freckles

At various times, and when the ingredients were available, I made valiant attempts at ridding myself of my hateful freckles. The treatments included everything from eating mass quantities of egg whites, to avoiding altogether all foods that had a tinge of orange in them, particularly carrots.

Lemon rinds were the hardest to come by, but were my favourite treatment. In the thirties, when Mother bought lemons for pie, it was because that Saturday she had received an especially good price for her eggs and chickens, and that wasn't to happen with any great frequency. The lemons were well-used by the time I ever got my hands on them. The juice would have been completely squeezed out for the pies, and then mother would sit for a few minutes with her elbows cupped in the half-lemon rinds. When she was sure they had done their job of whitening, I would claim them and rub them on my face until my skin smarted. Never once did I see any difference in the profusion of freckles on my face.

I also used whey, which I dabbed on with a face cloth. Once applied, I was forced to sit bolt upright in a chair with a towel around my neck to catch the drips. Buttermilk was also a favourite treatment, which met with about as much success as did the whey and the lemons.

In the summertime I sometimes used thin slices of cucumbers. This was a freckle cure my sister Audrey was sure would work, because Lilly Stolt from the Northcote School had ridden herself of warts with cucumbers. Lucky Lilly may have lost her warts, but the cucumbers did nothing for my hateful freckles.

Then one Saturday, a bitterly cold day as I remember, Emerson watched me cover myself with buttermilk and then stretch out on the old couch in the kitchen, resting while the 'treatment' did its work. He rarely gave me the time of day, but that morning he suggested if I stayed home he almost certainly had a cure for my freckles which he would be more than happy to pass along. Mother was getting the cutter ready to head into Renfrew for the week's supplies, which was a trip on which I usually accompanied her. I immediately agreed to stay at home, and Mother and my sister Audrey weren't out of the yard for more than a minute when Emerson flew into action.

He reasoned that if I tried all the cures at once, instead of hitting on each at different times, I would see remarkable results. The first thing he did was cover my face with egg whites. Then he rubbed on the heel of a week-old lemon peel that I had tucked away in my dresser drawer. After saturating a face cloth with buttermilk and warm whey, he slapped that on my face, leaving only enough space around my nose so that I could breathe.

I was standing beside the kitchen stove and wasn't having much luck in keeping the treatments on my face. Emerson hit on the idea that this mess should harden if it was to do any good, and the only place that was going to happen was outside on the back stoop. He threw his Mackinaw over my shoulders and shoved me through the back door, cautioning that I would have to stay there until my face felt good and stiff.

I was soon shivering in the freezing temperatures and attempted to get back in the kitchen, only to discover that Emerson had anticipated my move and thrown the bolt on the door. The egg whites froze first, then the whey and buttermilk, and then the tears that were streaming down my face. I pounded, I kicked and I threatened to go to the barn if I wasn't allowed back in the house immediately. Father would see what he had done to me, and he would be paying dearly. Emerson knew full well that I wouldn't traipse in my felt slippers through the waist-high snow to go out to the barn.

Finally, he decided that the treatment had been on my face long enough to work. He slammed open the bolt, put a crack in the door, and hauled me inside. My face was frozen solid. He had a basin of water waiting from the reservoir in the Findlay Oval, and he ordered me to wash the concoction off at once or else the treatment wouldn't do a bit of good.

It took some doing, but finally my face was cleaned—and smarting like a fresh cut. Emerson was standing there with Father's shaving mirror. Other than a beet-red face, I looked no different, and I wasted no time in telling Emerson. He insisted that a large freckle on the end of my nose was gone. He said he had noticed it particularly that morning at the breakfast table.

I desperately wanted to believe him, but I knew in my heart that I was doomed to have freckles the rest of my life. Emerson suggested we try the treatment again the next Saturday. Using a statement I had often heard Father use, the meaning of which was unclear to me, I said, "You'll see me in hell first."

Audrey's Diary

*M*y older sister Audrey liked her privacy. If I mistakenly put a pair of underwear in her drawer instead of mine, I heard about it in no uncertain terms. And heaven help me if she ever caught me in her bookbag, or as much as taking a peak inside her drawstring pencil case.

Needless to say, she was adamant that absolutely no one should ever take as much as a sidelong glance at her diary. It wasn't really a diary…not the kind my little friend Joyce Frances had with a tiny key and gold-edged pages. Both Audrey and I had big thick scribblers, and these were our diaries. Mother started us when we were very young, writing something every day in the scribblers. Even my three brothers, who thought the whole idea was sheer nonsense, had to make daily entries.

Audrey and I loved to hide ourselves in a corner of the kitchen at night and write our personal thoughts in our scribblers. I usually left my scribbler sitting on the parlour table. Not Audrey. She kept hers under her pillow—day and night.

There was an unwritten law in our house: no one was to put as much as a finger on Audrey's diary, or they would have Mother to deal with. The first thing Audrey would do in the morning was reach under her pillow to make sure no one had taken her diary through the night. Then she'd make up the bed, pulling the feather ticking up over her pillow, and she always gave the area a little pat, as if to say, "You're safe until I get home from school."

I was dying to look in the scribbler; however, Audrey assured me if I went against Mother's orders, there was a very good chance I would go blind. She knew several youngsters in Renfrew County who met just such a fate for disobeying a parent. I asked for names, but as usual Audrey's answer was, "Never mind…but that's a fact."

One day at Northcote School, Audrey's whole life was ruined. She wailed that she doubted it would ever be right again. The story went something like this… Unbeknownst to Audrey, Emerson stole her diary from under her pillow and took it to school in his bookbag. He gathered a bunch of boys behind the outdoor privy, and together they hooted and hollered over the contents of Audrey's very private writings.

The first Audrey knew what was going on was when Cecil came roaring out from around the back of the privy to stick his tongue out at her and defy her to prove that he did, in fact, have cheese for brains! Not a minute passed before Edward came charging across the schoolyard, adamantly denying he was madly in love with Iva…and what's more he had a good mind to go in and tell Miss Crosby all the terrible things Audrey had said about her. Audrey turned pure white…and then I could see the blood starting to rise in her cheeks. That meant she was roary-eyed mad. I always thought she was just about the prettiest girl at Northcote School, and her rosy cheeks, I thought, made her even more beautiful. At that moment, she was awfully pretty.

She made a beeline for Emerson who seemed intent on examining something that was in his hand. She caught him off-guard and wholloped him with such a bang that I was sure she had maimed him for life.

She demanded her diary. Emerson looked at her as if he had never laid eyes on her before in his life. She was taking another aim at him, and only his quickness to move aside saved him from her landing another punch in the vicinity of his head.

He pointed in the direction of the privy. We could hear giggles coming from the fence behind. Audrey began to move toward the sounds. I was close behind. I didn't want to miss one second of the excitement.

There lined up along the fence, like a row of pigeons, were all the entrance-class boys. Two-Mile Herman was in the middle, holding Audrey's diary, and reading from it in a high-pitched, exaggerated voice.

Audrey tore the book out of his hands and stomped into the school to hide it in her bookbag. Emerson avoided her glare for the rest of the day. She didn't dare tell Miss Crosby, since there was obviously something in the journal about her. I knew full well that Emerson was going to have to face the music sooner or later. Audrey, in fact, made him pay dearly that very day on the way home from school.

Audrey called him everything under the sun. Some of the names I had never heard before, but instinct told me she wouldn't repeat them in front of Mother. Finally she asked him why he would do such a dastardly deed. He dug deep in his pocket and brought out a handful of pennies. He said he had charged a cent a peek and made nine cents out of the whole deal. Audrey demanded the money, and as she was still spitting fire, Emerson handed it over as meek as a lamb. He knew to do otherwise would court disaster when he got home. Audrey said she was going to write the whole thing in her diary when she got home, so that future generations could see the kind of hairpin she had for a brother. Those were her exact words.

That night she wrote for ages in her journal. The nine pennies were tied into her hanky and put in the corner of her dresser drawer. The next day coming home from school, we stopped in at Briscoe's General Store and bought two ice cream cones with the money. She and I licked them right in front of Emerson, who knew better than to ask for even a taste.

Thanksgiving

I remember the year that Thanksgiving almost caused a riot, and threatened to put an end to the religious overtones of the occasion. It was the year I decided that if I ever saw another turkey as long as I lived, it would be too soon for me.

As usual, Uncle Johnny, Aunt Vanetta and all their children and grandchildren were expected. They were staunch Catholics and lived in Ottawa, so they would have to attend Mass and drive out after church. Mother said they wouldn't be at the farm until long after we got home from our own Lutheran church, seeing as how Aunt Vanetta wouldn't let Uncle Johnny drive over twenty-five miles an hour.

The day before Thanksgiving, the pumpkin pies were made and sitting out in the cold summer kitchen. The house had been scrubbed from top to bottom, and the stuffing was ready for the raisins, the chopped onions and the rubbed summer savoury. Everett was sent out to corner the gobbler and do what he had to do.

I had this terrible phobia about eating anything I had seen running around in the yard before it came in contact with the axe, so I didn't want to know any of the details. I knew if I did I wouldn't be able to swallow one mouthful of turkey.

I might have known my brother Emerson would have to put his two cents' worth into this whole affair. It began just after Everett was sent out to the drive shed. Since Mother had decided to add applesauce to our groaning table of Thanksgiving vittles, Emerson said he would sure like some help picking up the windfall apples behind the barn.

The request sounded simple enough, especially when Emerson said the job would go much faster if he held the bag while I climbed the tree and shook it to loosen the best apples. The rest would be gathered later and fed to the pigs. Mother had nodded in agreement when she saw this rare happening—my brother Emerson actually being nice to me for no earthly reason whatsoever. Not once did I stop to think that windfalls were on the ground, nor did I wonder why it was me who had to climb the tree to shake it.

We set out, with Emerson carrying the grain bag and me in my bare feet, because he said I could shinny up the tree easier that way. As we rounded the corner by the silo, there was Everett trying to corner the gobbler, who seemed to have a premonition of what was in store for him.

When we got to the apple tree, Emerson bent down on one knee, told me to climb on, and he hoisted me up into the lowest branch, which was still a fair distance from the ground. It was an easy job just to climb up, limb by limb, until I was right in the centre of the apple tree. Just as I was ready to shake, Emerson said he better go and help Everett corner the gobbler since he seemed a far way off from catching it. He said I would be perfectly all right where I was and not to move until he got back. As if I could go anywhere. The ground looked about two storeys below me, and I was sure my brother would never leave me stranded there for long.

Well, I was right. He didn't. But instead of helping Everett to corner the gobbler, which by this time was roary-eyed mad, Emerson let it out of the barnyard enclosure and chased it right over to the apple tree. Its wings were scraping the ground, its neck was blood red, and it was boxing at the boys as if its life depended on it, which of course it did.

I screamed that I wanted down, but the boys chose to ignore me. One got on one side of the apple tree and one on the other, and Emerson threw the grain sack over the gobbler, rendering it helpless. Everett carted it away, as it thrashed around in the bag. The roars, I'm sure, could be heard in Admaston, which was miles away.

Emerson thought it his everlasting duty to describe in minute detail exactly what Everett planned on doing to the gobbler on the chopping block behind the drive shed. I often found if I sang at the top of my lungs and plugged my ears, I could not only drown out the sounds around me,

I could take my mind off the issue at hand. So that's exactly what I did, much to my hateful brother's delight. He picked up what apples were scattered on the ground, piled them into a granite pan, and casually offered to help me down from the tree. I thought he deserved the same treatment as the gobbler, but I didn't dare say a word or I would have spent the rest of the afternoon in the upper reaches of the branches.

The next day, Emerson kept reminding me what the gobbler looked like just before it met its Waterloo. I hummed and plugged my ears. Even though it no longer remotely resembled the gobbler Everett had carried around behind the drive shed in a grain sack, I couldn't get a mouthful of it down—a fact which didn't go unnoticed by Emerson.

The cousins, aunts and uncles ate like it was their last meal on earth. And when they all piled into Uncle Johnny's Hupmobile to go back to Ottawa, I was delighted to see the last of the gobbler piled into a honey pail, along with a bag of freshly dug potatoes and carrots and a bucket of windfall apples, to make the trip back to the city with them.

Even though the old gobbler had a mean streak in him a mile wide, which made me skirt him every time I went near the barnyard, it still upset me to think of how he met his end. It actually sent shivers up my back, and sent my stomach into spasms.

It was a long time before I was able to relish a turkey dinner again, all of which further pleased my brother Emerson. Back then I had never heard of the word "vegetarian," but with the least encouragement, it wouldn't have taken much to turn me into one.

The Flea Circus

Mother talked endlessly about the sights of her beloved New York, including all the things you could do that didn't cost a penny, and of spectacles she was sure you could find nowhere else in the world. We hung onto every word, each one of us five children creating our own images of the glories of this great and wonderful city.

One occasion particularly comes to mind, and that was when our Lapointe cousins were visiting the farm from Montreal. It was a hot and sticky day. We had taken refuge in the grape arbour, all sitting around Mother who was in the big wooden swing. Someone was fanning her with a copy of the *Renfrew Mercury*, as she told of the wonders of New York City. Even young Ronny—that incorrigible cousin who wasn't easily impressed—was spellbound as she talked about trains that ran on tracks high above the streets, and a place called an automat, where you could buy your lunch for a dime from a little glass window in a wall.

Then, for the first time, she told us about a circus that even in our wildest imagination we couldn't fathom. It was a circus of fleas. She said they wore little harnesses, and their trainer showed them off in a magnified glass-top case. The fleas obeyed his every command. We couldn't imagine anything so fascinating.

Ronny's eyes started to slit. I could tell his fertile mind was working overtime and that he was hatching some plan that was bound to get him into trouble.

When story time was over, Mother went into the house, and we kids scattered…some to get cooled off in the Bonnechere and some to get a cup of ice-cold water from the well. Ronny sort of slinked off towards the barn. I never took my eyes off him. I knew he was up to something. He was walking slowly over the barnyard, stick in hand, poking the ground, eyes cast down with the deepest concentration.

Ronny finally found what he was looking for. It was a big black beetle. We called them June bugs, and they were in great abundance on the farm. I hated them with a passion.

I wasted no time in asking Ronny what he intended to do with it. Now his eyes were barely visible between the lashes. "I'm going to make a harness out of thread, and train this critter to perform, that's what I'm going to do," he said. "And I'm going to charge admission. Now, if you want to get to see it free, you better help me."

I took some thread out of Mother's sewing box. It was the heavy black thread she used for sewing buttons on our winter coats. Ronny had moved over to the back of the silo, so no one could see what he was doing. He figured if he could get the bug harnessed and trained before anyone saw him, he was more likely to get away with charging for the show. The beetle was helpless on its back, but I was still terrified to give it more than an occasional glance. Ronny fashioned a harness of sorts from the thread and wrapped it around its gyrating body. Then he flipped it over on a rock, and with a small twig prepared to embark it on its education. It scurried in every direction, and each time Ronny would bring it back to a starting position.

This went on in the beating sun for what seemed like hours to me. I was anxious to get on with other things, and was reaching the conclusion that Ronny was never going to teach this beetle a thing. Every time I started to move away, Ronny hauled me back to hold the harness. It became a battle of wills between the beetle and my Montreal cousin, and it very much looked like this was one war Ronny was not going to win.

I might have known Ronny was not going to give up easily on what could be a lucrative venture. He dispatched me to the house to fetch the rest of the kids, and they were all to bring a cent with them if they wanted to see this spectacle. I had no idea what they were going to see for a cent, but I did exactly as I was told.

Everyone lined up beside the plank Ronny had arranged for the show, and he extracted a cent from every outstretched hand. Then he took the bug out of his hand and set it on the board. It never moved a fraction of an inch. He touched it with a finger, then with a blade of grass. Finally he blew on it. It was either asleep or dead. Seven pairs of eyes were glued to the beetle. Nothing happened. Emerson wanted his money back. So did Audrey. Everett said he was going to the house to tell Mother, who had no tolerance for inhumane actions towards animals.

Ronny knew he had to do something, or he was going to have to give back the pennies he had collected. "Now I ask you," he said, "have you ever seen a bug in a harness?" We all agreed we hadn't. "Have you ever seen a harness that small?" Again, we all said no. "Then that's what you've paid for. You've seen two things today you've never seen before—the tiniest harness in Renfrew County...and a bug tied into it." He dusted off his knees, left the motionless bug where it was, rattled the coins in his pocket and headed for the pump for a drink. "I'd say, you've got your money's worth," he said without looking back.

Leap Year

As far as Mother and Father were concerned, Audrey certainly wasn't old enough to have a boyfriend. "After all," Mother said, "she is barely seventeen." "She has plenty of time for that nonsense," added Father from his position of authority in the rocking chair by the oven door.

Audrey had a different idea. After all, she was in the entrance class at the Northcote School, and just about every girl her age was going to the Saturday night dances.

Audrey was sitting at the kitchen table pretending to be leafing through the Eaton's catalogue. I knew differently. She wasn't really looking at all, she was listening, just to see if there was a change in Mother's or Father's position. She waited for just the right moment and then she announced to everyone within earshot that this was leap year. Since I was only seven, I was not familiar with the term, and couldn't for the life of me figure out what a special year had to do with going to the Saturday night dance.

Audrey said that in leap year the girls were allowed to ask any one of the neighbourhood boys to the dances. I thought that was a wonderful idea, but Emerson argued that no one in their right mind would go out with a girl who had to stoop to asking a boy for a date. Audrey argued that it wouldn't really be a date. Father wondered, if it wasn't a date, what in the world would you call it. Audrey rolled her eyes to the ceiling and made a terrible face behind the Eaton's catalogue.

"Besides," she said in a most pathetic voice, trying to get the most sympathy she could, "there are lots of old people who go to the Saturday night dances. All our neighbours are as old as the hills...some of them are as old as you and Father," she said in Mother's direction. "So it wouldn't be as if we were alone."

By the time we were ready for bed, Audrey had wangled an agreement out of Mother that she could ask someone to go to the Saturday night dance...but just this once, and only because it was leap year. Right away Emerson and Everett wondered who she was going to ask. "I'll bet it's that loony Two-Mile Herman," Emerson said of a young neighbour lad from down the road. Everett said he doubted very much that he would go with Audrey, since he had the sweets for a girl name Lena. Audrey glared at both of them, and pranced upstairs to bed. I was right behind her. I couldn't wait to see who she was going to ask.

When we both crawled between the feather tickings, Audrey confided to me that she had already asked a boy by the name of Patrick. I asked her why she hadn't said so downstairs. She said she didn't want to press her luck because Patrick was a Catholic. I had no idea what his religion had to do with leap year, but I kept my thoughts to myself.

It was the next night that Audrey announced she had invited Patrick to the Saturday night dance, and he had accepted. She said she was expected to pick him up in the cutter, take him to the dance, provide his lunch, and take him home later. It sounded to me like more bother than it was worth. She waited for Father or Mother to say something, but all Mother said was, "That's nice, dear."

Audrey was walking on air for the rest of the week. When Saturday rolled around cold and crisp, she said she would like to leave at seven o'clock. Father agreed that would be a good time, since she had two concessions to travel to pick up Patrick.

Audrey came downstairs just before seven. She was wearing silk stockings, and I could smell Lily of the Valley talcum powder clear across the room. "Get your coats on, children," Mother said. We looked puzzled and Audrey looked thunderstruck. "Don't forget your lunch, Audrey," she added, and then she grabbed a basket, which was obviously for the rest of us to eat at the dance. Audrey looked like she had been cemented to the kitchen floor. At this point, there was nothing much she could do. She could either accept all of us along for the ride, or she could stay home.

We piled into the sleigh, Audrey glum and silent, the rest of us excited. There was no opportunity for anything more than a handshake when we dropped Patrick off after the dance. Audrey was sitting up front in the sleigh with Mother and Father, the rest of us were in the back. I asked Everett if that's all there was to a date. He said he guessed it would depend on whether your whole family was along. I wondered why we did go. Everett looked up at the stars and said, "I guess it has something to do with leap year. I heard some boys go real crazy in leap year." "Don't be silly, Everett," Emerson said. "We all went because Patrick is a Catholic." Neither explanation seemed quite right to me. For the life of me, I couldn't understand what Patrick's religion had to do with the whole family going to pick him up in the sleigh.

Audrey said she didn't care if leap year went on until the next century, she would never ask another boy to go to the Saturday night dance as long as she lived. "I have never been so embarrassed in my whole life. Imagine, seven of us going to pick up a date. I hope he doesn't tell anyone at the Northcote School," she lamented.

Mother said that was sheer nonsense, and there were plenty of nice neighbour boys who Audrey might consider asking at a later date. As far as Audrey was concerned, she would probably end up a spinster just like old Cora. She lived all alone in an old log shack on the corner of a neighbour's farm. Father said those neighbours had given Cora the piece of property because she never married and had no one to fend for her.

I mulled this over in my fertile mind. If Audrey never married, and it was all because the entire family insisted on being with her when she picked up a date, what would happen to me when I was old enough to ask someone to the Saturday night dances? I thought of all the hateful boys at the Northcote School, and those neighbourhood boys who were friends of my brothers and who loved to tease me about my freckles and red hair. I decided right then and there, there wasn't one of them I would give two pieces of straw for. Maybe old Cora wasn't so dumb after all. I fell asleep that night wondering what corner of the farm I would build a log cabin on.

Looking a Gift Horse in the Mouth

Mother said Aunt Freda would have to be demented. Surely she should know that the farm she grew up on still didn't enjoy the amenities she enjoyed in Chicago. Amenities like electricity and running water.

Goodness knows Aunt Freda came to visit often enough that she would know what improvements Father had been able to make…and they didn't include electric wires from the Northcote Side Road and indoor plumbing. We counted ourselves lucky the day we were able to run telephone poles down our long lane to hook up with Central. Between the Hines', one farm over, and us, we were able to get both lines to come in on the same poles and wires. Our Uncle Lou thought it was terrible that we had no phone, and it was through his generosity that we finally were able to connect to Central any time we wanted to make a call, either in the Northcote area, or even as far as Renfrew if the need arose.

Now, Aunt Freda should have known all this, but she still phoned to Briscoe's General Store at Northcote where Mr. Briscoe had to phone us and relay messages. She still also sent us parcels that needed both running water and electricity. Parcels which were completely useless to us and which caused Mother, each time something foolish arrived, to declare once again that Aunt Freda was demented.

Sometimes Aunt Freda even sent us things we couldn't figure out. This was like the day a big box arrived for us at the station in Renfrew. The express office phoned to ask us to get it out as soon as possible because the box was as big as a piano.

Excitement was running pretty high that day as Father hitched up the team of horses and, with five children in tow, headed into Renfrew. It was an awfully big box, all right. Tied with heavy rope, it had Father's and Mother's name written on the side with black crayon. As soon as Father lifted it, we knew it wasn't a piano. He could just about handle it with one hand. He heaved it on the wagon, and we headed home with what we were sure was going to be a wonderful treasure.

It didn't take Everett all day to rip into the box when it was set down in the middle of the kitchen. We thought it was all newspapers because it was absolutely full of scrunched up sections of a Chicago daily. By the time Everett reached the treasure, the kitchen floor was littered with papers.

Finally, he hauled out an apparatus, the like of which we had never seen before. It stood about two feet high with a long handle and reams of electrical cord wrapped around and around a spoke sticking out from the side. It had a big canvas bag hanging under the handle, and when Mother saw it, she just shook her head. "A vacuum cleaner. Now I ask you. What in heaven's name good is an electric vacuum cleaner out here in Northcote?"

Audrey and I had to ask what it was used for, and Mother gave us a quick lesson while she was tucking the vacuum cleaner back in the box. Father was actually showing an interest in the thing. He hauled it back out, set it in the middle of the floor, circled it a couple of times, and said. "Yup. I think I have a use for this danged thing." No one could imagine what he had in mind. We were to find out soon enough when Saturday rolled around and we headed into town for our week's supplies and with the vacuum cleaner sitting by Father on the wagon seat.

He headed right for the home of Mrs. Stewart, one of Renfrew's most prominent dowagers. We children were not allowed to go to the door with Father, but were warned to be on our best behaviour. We could see Father and Mrs. Stewart in animated conversation, and finally Father headed back to the wagon and lifted the electric vacuum cleaner off the seat. He vanished into the house with the big oak and glass door and in a few minutes came out with something tucked under his arm. It had legs on it, and looked very much like a parlour table. When he got closer to the wagon, we could see "Singer" written on the side of the machine in gold letters. Father said nothing, but started up the horses. After getting our supplies, he aimed the horses for the Northcote Road.

Only when we got into the kitchen did Father tell us what he had done. He had talked Mrs. Stewart into swapping her pedal sewing machine for the new electric vacuum cleaner.

He was very pleased with himself, and with some shifting around in the kitchen, he found a place for it under a window. To complete the effect, he took a geranium off the cupboard and plunked it down in the centre of the machine. Mother, who we thought would be delighted, looked at Father and said, "But Albert, I already have a treadle sewing machine. It's old, I know, but it works." Then she repeated…"I already have a machine." Father rubbed his sleeve over the top of the new machine and said, "That's all right, Mrs. Stewart already has a vacuum cleaner."

A Year of Good Luck

That was the year that, for some unexplained reason, Aunt Lizzie from Regina had brought her usual winter hand-me-down box with her, instead of sending it to us on the CPR train. My father's sister, although good to us in many ways, nonetheless caused great upheaval in our home whenever she came for a visit...which according to my father was much too often. She was domineering and tried many times to make Father into a sophisticated farmer, which was beyond even her capabilities. Father would always remain a simple man of the soil, who plodded along at farming as best he could and in his own fashion. He made it clear that Aunt Lizzie could keep her newfangled ideas in Regina.

At any rate, that New Year's Eve day started out like any other in the week. There were no plans for any celebrations. On past New Year's Eves, Mother had let us stay up after nine o'clock and we had had hot chocolate before we went to bed. Sometimes we sang while she played the harmonica, but that was usually the extent of recognizing that one year was about to end and another was ready to begin.

That year, Aunt Lizzie took it upon herself to celebrate in her own style. That meant Mother had to invite some of the neighbours in, and the afternoon was spent making sandwiches and a big chocolate layer cake. We children were quite excited. To have company in the middle of the week in itself was a landmark event. Father thought the whole idea was nonsense, but he took the line of least resistance and sat back and let Mother and Aunt Lizzie plan the evening.

Instead of getting into our pyjamas after supper, we were sent upstairs by Aunt Lizzie and told to get into our next-to-Sunday-best outfits, comb our hair and tidy the bedrooms, because you never knew who might wander upstairs. It would never do to have strangers see clothes lying around, or an unmade bed.

We had barely finishing redding up the kitchen when a knock came to the back door. Aunt Lizzie patted her hair in place and flew across the kitchen before anyone else could get out of their chair. There stood Uncle Alec Thom, the full of the door, with his fiddle tucked under his arm. "You can't come in. You can't come in," she cackled. She put her arm up to stop him from taking another step. Father got up to intervene, but Aunt Lizzie held her ground. She snatched off Uncle Alec's hat. "We can't have someone with black hair be the first person to cross the threshold, that would mean a year of bad luck. I'm afraid you will have to wait until some fair-haired man comes along." Father was starting to lose his temper. "Alec, you come right in," and he swung the door wide. Aunt Lizzie braced her body against the door jam. It was obvious she meant business. Father said he never heard of such nonsense and that it must be some crazy notion Aunt Lizzie had brought from the west. Nonetheless, Aunt Lizzie was determined. The first person over the threshold was going to be someone with fair hair, and then we would have good luck for the entire next year. Uncle Alec said as far as he was concerned he had been invited fair and square, and if Lizzie thought he was going to stand freezing in the woodshed until someone with fair hair came along, she had another thought coming.

My sister Audrey suggested our brother Everett, who was as fair as a lily, go outside and come back in and that would be the same thing. Aunt Lizzie thought for a minute and then said, "No that wouldn't do."

Mother was hissing over by the stove and slamming the big galvanized kettle around. She did that when she was hopping mad. She was muttering under her breath how foolish she had been to ask Aunt

Lizzie to stay beyond Christmas. "Nonsense…that's what it is, plain nonsense."

Uncle Alec probably would have stood in the woodshed until morning, arguing with Aunt Lizzie, had not another sleigh pulled into the yard. We all ran to the window when we heard the sleigh bells, and Mother was heard to say, "I hope to heavens it's the Briscoes…they all have red hair."

It turned out to be Mr. Hines from next door. He didn't have a hair on his head, and Aunt Lizzie had a hard time determining if he was qualified to be the first to step over the threshold. Father said he was as fair as a lily, always had been, never knew him to have a dark hair. Aunt Lizzie bowed low, and our neighbour swept in, followed quickly by Uncle Alec who said *he* was a hair's breadth from heading home. I whispered to Mother that I remembered how Mr. Hines used to have jet-black hair before he lost it all with a fever. "Be quiet, Mary," Mother said. "Let's get this night over with before I lose my mind, and then we *really* will have bad luck all next year."

Northcote

For reasons I have never been able to explain, I avoided going back to Northcote for many years. Was it the fear of losing the mystique I had built up surrounding my old homestead and the places which played such a prominent role in my stories? Did I harbour a fear of disillusionment? Or had it more to do with the fact that both my parents were gone, and I had a deep-seated concern that returning to the old homestead, the general store and the Northcote School would fill me with longing and sadness? Perhaps it was a combination of all of those things.

One day, however, a CBC assignment took me down the Northcote Side Road, now officially named Highway 60. I saw the ditches filled with water. The very ditches my little friend Velma and I walked in on our way home from school, with our navy blue, fleece-lined bloomers with the tight elastic legs holding our skirts tucked up inside and away from the water. And wasn't that Briscoe's General Store? Looking down the Rink Road, wasn't that the Northcote School I could see in the distance?

It was decades since I had been down that road, and that day, with a spring rain pelting against my windshield, I was filled with a sadness I had never experienced before. What had happened to Velma? Had she married? Did she have a family? Through misty eyes, I remembered how close we were as young friends. My first experience with feather tickings on a bed were at Velma's house. My introduction to old-time fiddle music was through her father, whom we Haneman children called Uncle Alec. I was able to bring to mind a picture of her mother, Aunt Bertha, with her soft brown hair rolled in a coil at the back of her head, and I could once again see her face and hear her gentle German voice. Next-door neighbours, the Thom family were as much a part of our lives as were the Bonnechere River, the sugar bush, and even Central, the telephone switchboard operator who could connect us, inexplicably, to the outside world. And Velma Thom was my closest friend.

That day I drove on, not sure where I was going, only knowing that my producer had sent me in this direction. I passed construction crews working in rain-slicked orange plastic coats, and farms unfamiliar with the passing of time. For some reason, however, I couldn't get my little friend Velma out of my mind. Finally, I realized, although I was sure I hadn't left the Northcote Side Road, that I was hopelessly lost. I could have stopped and asked directions from any number of road workers, but still I drove on as if an unknown force was in charge of my destiny.

I drove into a farm lane with a large brick house facing the road, and nosed my car as close to the sweeping verandah as I could in order to made a dash for the door. My neck was stiff from the long drive, which I was sure had taken me well past my appointed destination.

The door was opened before I had a chance to rap. Standing there, tall and stately, with the same brown hair as Aunt Bertha, was a woman who knew at once that I was hopelessly lost. She was so much like Aunt Bertha that I wondered if perhaps I had wandered into another dimension and was, in fact, being catapulted back to that other time. She asked me where I was going, and I froze as the memory of Aunt Bertha's voice came to me, just as if she were standing in front of me. But that would be impossible. She would be a very old lady by then, if she was alive at all. When the woman saw how stunned I was, unable to speak, she asked, "Are you all right? Is there something wrong?" I found my voice and said, "Are you any relation to someone I knew many years ago? A woman by the name of Bertha Thom?"

With the same German accent I remembered so well, she softly answered, "I am her daughter Velma." As I wept with emotions I could not understand, I said "I'm Mary Haneman."

What took me past dozens of other farms, and road workers, directly into the one farm on that highway that would lead me to my little friend of another time? Fate? Perhaps. That day, the fear of "going home" was erased. I have since been able to return many times to revisit the old farm, renew my friendship with dear Velma, and go back to the Northcote School. Since then, the old homestead has changed hands, Briscoe's General Store has closed and become a residence, the Northcote School has been made into a community centre, and dear Velma, although we didn't know it at the time, was already in the throes of an aggressive cancer, succumbing to this dreadful disease almost three years to the day from our reacquaintance.

Since that first trip back to Northcote, I have become reunited with other past school friends, Allen and Joyce Francis. Very rich, indeed, did I think the Francis' were. After all, they lived in a brick house and ours was log. They took store-bought meat to school on their sandwiches, and ours were jam.

Although I never did know the rich history of the community called Northcote, Allen Francis and his wife Shirley have been able to fill in the many blanks for this book. It was certainly a shock when Allen told me that there never was an official place called Northcote. Yet everyone for miles around knew it to be there. It was simply known by that name as . part of the tradition of that part of the Ottawa Valley. Allen said it was part English and part French in origin, actually meaning "north side." We knew Northcote as the place where Briscoe's General Store was located. A few miles away was the Northcote School, and certainly we always called the road the Northcote Side Road before the province got fancy and tagged it Highway 60!

At one time, Northcote was a busy community. There was an apiary, a sawmill, a cheese factory, and at least three silver fox ranches. According to Allen Francis, Northcote became famous for its fine herds of Holstein cattle. Two of these herds were actually designated Master-Breeder herds, as the finest in the land, by the Holstein Association of Canada.

The Northcote School was built in 1927. Constructed of cinder blocks, it was considered quite grand by the standards of the day. So progressive was the school that during the fall and winter months, the children were served hot lunches to add to what was brought from home. Allen remembers the senior classes as having to not only serve the meal but wash up after.

I'm afraid I don't remember the hot lunches, but I do remember the day my brother Emerson was sent home in disgrace for taking a garter snake into the school in his pocket, terrifying all of us girls, including Miss Crosby. I sat with crimson cheeks as I listened to my brother being chastised by the teacher and ordered out of the school for the rest of the day.

The first time I went back to the Northcote School, I looked in stunned amazement at its size. It was so very small inside. The blackboards still went across the front and down the north side, but I remembered the classroom as being very large. I wondered if it had been remodelled when it was turned into a community centre. I was assured that it hadn't been altered.

I recall the Northcote School as a safe haven. Wasn't this where Miss Crosby kept all of us under her watchful eye? There was no taunting allowed. Everyone at the Northcote School, regardless of his or her parents' station in the community, was treated the same. We all had purpose, and in Miss Crosby's eyes at least, our affluence, or lack of it, had absolutely nothing to do with how we were treated.

We had a healthy respect for the teacher in those days. Her word was law! Fair to a fault, she nevertheless ruled with an iron arm and the sparing use of the long black strap that hung on a cup hook from the side of her desk. All she had to do was cast an eye in its direction, and even the big Senior Fourth boys, who towered over her, would cringe.

I can go back to both Northcote and the school today and feel nostalgic but not sad anymore. It took time to sort everything into its proper place in my memory, but once I had done that, I was able to see the community and the school for what they were and what they had become. Both were a vital part of my growing up. And today, after renewing friendships made so many years ago, I can see the community of Northcote as it has evolved. It is still full of names like Brisco (I have no idea why some spell it with an "e" and some don't), Manka, Thom, Francis, Elliott and Kallies. Many new families have also moved into the community. They will, as we and our neighbours did so many years ago, add vitality and warmth to this place they call home.

I don't suppose I am that different from others who have moved away from their homestead and yet feel a deep kinship to it. For me, Northcote, and especially the Northcote School, will always hold a special place in my heart and in my memories.

Treasures Between the Covers

I can't remember there being any more than two books in the Northcote School. One was a big black dictionary, the second a very worn, leather-bound bible. They both sat on the corner of Miss Crosby's desk. Apart from the few readers and spellers each pupil had, there were no other books in sight.

Miss Crosby would bring a storybook to school from her own collection every Friday. She would read a chapter to us each week, then she would take the book home again. Mother thought it was a disgrace that the Northcote School did not have a proper library, but there was little she could do about it. There certainly wasn't much money to buy books for her own children, let alone for the one-room country schoolhouse. Nonetheless, she always seemed to find a few extra pennies every birthday and Christmas to give each of her five children a small book. It meant she had to work especially hard to make enough sticky buns and homemade butter to peddle in Renfrew to earn a few extra dollars. When there were no other gifts in sight, we could always count on having a new book of our very own on those two special days each year.

I'm not sure now, so many years later, how Mother found out there was only one dictionary in the Northcote School. She thought every child should have his or her own. She even went so far as to suggest to

Miss Crosby that the inspector be approached for free copies. Teachers quaked in their shoes when the inspector came to the school, so needless to say, Miss Crosby wasn't the least receptive to the idea of asking him for dictionaries.

No, the children would just have to get along with the one that sat on the corner of her desk. Mother said she knew for a fact that every child in the town school had his or her own dictionary, and just because we lived in the country, we shouldn't be denied the privilege. As Miss Crosby couldn't be swayed on the issue, Mother set out to correct this injustice herself. Emerson was the first one of us to have a birthday following Mother's discussion with Miss Crosby. I suppose she figured that was as good a time as any to start us on the road to being equal to the town kids. When Emerson opened his present, there was the usual storybook, always a classic, and tied to the same parcel was a brand-new dictionary.

I remember it so well. It wasn't any bigger than a slice of bread. Thicker of course, and it was bright red with silver printing on the outside. It had the roughest paper I had ever witnessed in a book. I looked at the dictionary with envy, but I'm not at all sure Emerson was thrilled with the present. Mother made him write his name on the inside...just in case, she said, anyone got any bright ideas at the Northcote School. We all knew exactly what she meant. She made a paper cover for it out of newspaper to keep it fresh, and it was tucked into Emerson's canvas bookbag with his scribblers.

The next day Emerson wasn't long in showing everyone his new dictionary. Even Miss Crosby said it was mighty nice and would go a long way in improving Emerson's spelling. Miss Crosby was high on proper grammar and spelling.

As each of us had a birthday roll around, Mother would buy the usual book, and in the package would be the little red dictionary with the silver printing. Within the year, the five of us had our own dictionaries.

The brothers never thought of the dictionaries as proper birthday presents, but my sister Audrey and I knew how hard Mother had to work to get extra money to buy them. After all, they cost seventy-five cents at the Rexall Drug Store. With eggs selling at ten cents a dozen, and sticky buns going for a quarter, I know now how long it must have taken Mother to gather enough money to buy five brand-new dictionaries.

As my birthday was in December, I was the very last one to get my little red dictionary. When I was handed my present, it was a special occasion for me. I was filled with excitement, even though I knew exactly what was going to be in the parcel with my other book. At last, we all had our own dictionaries that had a place of honour on our desks at the Northcote School. Just like the kids in Renfrew.

Heads Above Everyone Else

We used to think head lice only attacked those children at the Northcote School who didn't practise everyday cleanliness and good hygiene. At least that was what Mother said. Well, we soon learned it had little to do with cleanliness and hygiene, and a great deal to do with whose head you came in contact with. Just like the winter flu or the spring fever, we could all expect, at one time or another during the school year, to come down with head lice.

Miss Crosby seemed to have a secret antenna which alerted her as to when she should go over each head with a fine-tooth comb—and that's exactly what she did. The search could come about from a simple gesture of someone scratching his head. That's all it took for Miss Crosby to go into her desk drawer and haul out the little white comb. There seemed to be no shame attached to the exercise, but rather it was just part of Miss Crosby's routine.

Starting with the youngest, she would march us up to a high stool at the front of the classroom. This was the same stool Cecil spent much of his time on…facing the east corner of the room where the two rows of blackboards met. Then, she would take the fine-tooth comb and go over our heads, peering at each bunch of hair stretched out in her hand. Those of us who were infected were ordered to the back row, and those of us who were clean, as Miss Crosby called the rest of us, were warned not to go near those who had been sent to the back of the room. After each head was searched, Miss Crosby would go to the wash basin at the side of the classroom, wash the comb with a brush, and then attack the next head.

It wasn't unusual for a whole family to be sent to the back of the room. And whether or not Miss Crosby found anything, we were all given notes to take home to our mother, telling her if head lice had turned up or not. If the note said we were infected, we were ordered to have a treatment immediately. Even those of us who were deemed clean were to have the treatment, just as a precaution. This didn't seem fair to my sister Audrey and me, especially since the treatment for girls was so different than that given to boys.

Just like every other essential of the day, each home had an array of fine-tooth combs. As soon as the note arrived from Miss Crosby, Audrey and I knew what we were in for. First, we had our hair washed with homemade lye soap. Then we had it washed again with a strong solution of coal oil and water.

We had to hold a wet face cloth over our eyes and nose, but that did little to protect us from the fumes. The coal oil stung like iodine in a raw cut, and I confess now that I roared at the top of my lungs from the first minute of the treatment until Mother was finished. I always marvelled at how my sister Audrey took the punishment without a whimper.

Once our heads had been scalded with the coal oil, we were then washed again with homemade soap, and finally our hair was rinsed with vinegar right out of the big gallon jug. This torture was repeated for about three nights in a row, and I wonder now at how we had any hair left when the final treatment was over.

The boys got off much easier. Their heads were washed and rinsed with vinegar, and then Mother sat them on a chair with a sheet around their necks. Using the clippers, their entire heads were shaved right down to the skin. They were as shiny as billiard balls when Mother was finished. The fallen hair was then gathered up and fed into the cookstove just in case there were any stray nits walking around alive.

Miss Crosby treated the outbreak just as she would if we had all taken the measles. It seems to me now, that no one was spared from either the head lice or the measles back in the thirties. None of us ever stayed home from school because we had head lice, but our mothers were expected to "clean the heads," as Miss Crosby called it, with a sense of urgency, as was stated in her notes home.

There were no fancy names for the affliction as there are today. Nobody liked getting head lice, especially since it was the torturous treatment that we dreaded more than the affliction. Unless my memory fails me, contracting the parasites had very little to do with any lack of basic hygiene. It did, however, have everything to do with being in too close contact in a one-room schoolhouse where everything was shared.

Edna Jean

Edna Jean looked strange. My sister Audrey said she worked at looking the way she did, but I didn't believe that for a minute. She was born that way. Edna Jean was tall and lanky, with a body like a flat board. Her hair was wild and jet black, and her skin was white and pasty. She always looked like she was just getting over a serious illness.

If the truth were known, she scared the starch out of me. Even though she was only my sister's age, she told fortunes, or pretended to. She said she could see what was going to happen long before the event and could tell what was going on in people's minds just by looking at them. This gave me great pause. When I had to confront her, I made awfully sure I was saying over and over in my mind, "Isn't she pretty" or "What lovely hair," even though deep in my heart I was thinking the absolute opposite.

It was thought she could put a hex on you too, if the spirit moved her. She claimed she was completely responsible for the mess of warts Orville developed, put there because he dared call her a beanpole with black sheep's wool glued to the top.

At any rate, we all had great respect for Edna Jean. Actually, it was more like fear. She always said if you were travelling to town and met someone walking on the road who had red hair, you should turn around immediately and go home. Since I had flaming red hair, I wondered where that put me. She said as long as *I* didn't meet another redhead I was fine, which greatly put my mind at ease. Another of her favourite myths was that if you met a wagonload of hay, you should never take a second look at it. Look at it once, and then turn your head so that your eyes would never come in contact with it again. Now, if you made a wish on the wagon of hay, you didn't have a hope in Halifax of the wish coming true if by accident you saw the hay a second time. Since our back road always seemed to have wagons of hay going and coming, I spent most of the time walking to school or driving into Renfrew with my eyes scrunched tight, or travelling backwards.

Edna Jean also put a lot of faith in a full moon. My brother Emerson said she went pure rangy when the moon was full, and how he would know I have no idea. Edna Jean said that when you first saw the full moon, you should face it, turn around three times and then make a wish, and it was bound to come true. Then you had to walk backwards into the house, or you could just forget the wish. We were also informed that you should never sleep with the moon shining on your face. Very bad luck, said Edna Jean.

We soon came to realize that, according to Edna Jean, just about everything around us was either a bad sign or a good one, and there wasn't much in between. We believed her wholeheartedly, even though I must say Edna Jean was awfully short on specific examples.

The older boys at the Northcote School thought the key to her lock turned the wrong way, which was another way of saying she was a little short of grey matter. They tried every which way to trap her, but Edna Jean always seemed to come out on top.

She was especially fond of predicting the weather. When the sun was bright and there wasn't a cloud in the sky, she had the habit of saying it would rain before dark, and invariably, the clouds would start to roll in as we were getting out of school. My brother Everett said she always made that prediction when the spring rains were expected anyway. He didn't put much faith in Edna Jean.

One day she told us it was very bad luck to walk on the left-hand side of the road going or coming to school. You always had to walk on the same side as your right hand. Well, the boys caught wind of this, and that day on the way home, they defied Edna Jean and marched along the left-hand side of the road singing, "Mean, mean, Edna Jean, homely as sin and twice as lean." All Edna Jean said was, "You'll see."

Well, call it faith, or call it an Edna Jean spell, or call it an over energetic bunch of farm boys, but to this day no one can say how it happened. While going over a culvert in the Northcote Road, my brother Earl either slipped or was pushed, and he rolled off the road, hitting his leg on the cement culvert. He lay in the ditch water as white as a sheet.

My sister Audrey gave no thought to being on the wrong side of the road and rushed over to assess the damage. The damage was a broken leg and a week in the Renfrew hospital. Emerson said it was an accident plain and simple. Edna Jean was reluctant to take the full responsibility, but after Mother and Father came to fetch Earl, and the rest of us continued the walk home, there wasn't one of us who didn't move over to the right side of the road.

Cecil Caps It

Cecil was never the same after that trip to Pembroke. He was gone for several days, and of course that meant he wasn't at school, which in itself was a landmark occasion. Cecil never missed school. We never did know the exact reason he was away, but it had something to do with his mother having to look after a houseful of relatives who had come down with 'the grip,' as it was called back then. The rumour went that Cecil's father flatly refused to have the responsibility of caring for Cecil, so his mother was forced to take him to Pembroke on her trip of mercy.

When he came back, after several days of absence, he certainly was changed. My brother Emerson said he had become citified, and that didn't sit too well with the other boys of the Northcote School.

One thing I noticed different about him was he had given up his gum rubbers for a pair of running shoes. That meant he couldn't crack his toes any longer during school hours. This was a great relief to Miss Crosby, who was constantly glaring at him when he indulged in his favourite pastime. Emerson said replacing the foot gear was a dead giveaway that Cecil had changed since his trip to Pembroke. Each day after he returned, Cecil introduced another transformation. He started by wearing a navy and white bandana around his neck, tucked into his plaid, flannel shirt. No boy ever wore a bandana around his neck! He took a razing on that first day, but nobody razed Cecil and got away with it. The boy who dared poke fun at him ended up with a bloody nose. The teasing stopped and the bandana stayed.

Then about a week after Cecil returned from his trip to Pembroke, he came to school with his hair slicked back and his bib overalls exchanged for a pair of breeks. The only time we ever saw Cecil in breeks was at church on Sunday.

"Nobody wears bib overalls on the streets in Pembroke," Cecil said as he straightened his bandana. He took off his windbreaker and hung it on his hook at the back of the room. When he turned around we just about keeled over. All over his plaid shirt were KIK bottle caps. He looked like a walking billboard for Briscoe's General Store.

Nobody said a word. I had never seen so many KIK bottle caps in my life. They marched down his left side and up his right. Emerson was the first to break the silence. "Sure have a lot of bottle caps on your shirt there, Cecil. How do you keep them there anyway?"

Cecil was delighted to be able to demonstrate how the whole exercise was accomplished. He had a pocketful of caps which he had yet to attach to his shirt and which he spread out on the lunch table. Then he took his jackknife out of his pocket, made sure every eye in the Nortchote School was upon him, opened the blade, and pried out the little round disk of cork that was inside each cap.

He reached over to Emerson and opened the top two buttons of his flannel shirt. He put the cork under his shirt and the cap on top of it and pushed the cork into place. The cap stuck solid. Emerson was beaming like a Coleman lamp.

"Say, that's just about the cleverest thing I ever saw," Emerson said, all smiles. We all wanted a cork and cap fastened to our person, but there weren't enough to go around. Miss Crosby thought the frivolity had gone on long enough and she rapped her desk a few times with the pointer which brought us all to order.

Well, I never saw so much excitement over a new fad. We haunted Briscoe's General Store and begged our mother to buy KIK with her weekly supplies, which was like asking for a pair of patent-leather shoes to wear to school. The few caps we were able to gather marched up and down our sweaters like war medals. Sometimes the corks would break and the cap would fall to the floor. This development, in fact, led to the end of the KIK-cap fad when Miss Crosby one day announced the fad was over. There would be no more soft-drink caps worn in the Northcote School, and that was final. I think we were all glad the exercise was over. It was getting to the point where everyone was trying to outdo everyone else.

Cecil went back to wearing his bib overalls, the bandana was moved to his back pocket for a handkerchief, the running shoes were replaced with gum rubbers, and he went back to cracking his toes. The Northcote School was back to normal.

The Uninvited

Distractions from our daily routine at the Northcote School simply were not tolerated. Miss Crosby insisted every one of us pay the strictest attention to our schoolwork, and our eyes were not allowed to wander. Our strict but kindly teacher kept us so busy there really wasn't much time to look at anything other than our school books or the blackboard anyway. In the dead of winter, all we could see out the window was endless bare trees and snow, so there wasn't much to grab our attention there. If Miss Crosby was lecturing someone, it was as much as your life was worth to take your eyes off your workbook and glance at the offending pupil. Even if someone fell out of his desk, which Gerald did with regularity, no one dared turn around to see if he had been knocked unconscious!

When the winter had closed around us, it was doubly hard to concentrate at the Northcote School. The baseboards, which ran around the entire outer walls of the room, had holes in them here and there, where several times a day a mouse would peek out, scurry around the perimeter of the room and dash into the nearest escape hatch. Either Miss Crosby never saw the mice before that fateful day or she figured, like the rest of us girls, that if we ignored them, they would go away.

I remember it was bitterly cold. The windowpanes were so frosted we couldn't see outside. The old stove crackled, and the smell of felt inner soles drying out on the pieces of wood by the fire filled the air. The seat of the desk I shared with Velma was like a block of ice, and our felt-slippered feet were numb from the cold. Velma pushed my side gently with her elbow. One finger of her hand pointed towards the outside wall near Miss Crosby's desk, and I followed her lowered eyes to a hole in the baseboard. A field mouse, with only its head showing, was about to make its entrance into the room.

Miss Crosby's purse, a big, black leather affair, sat on the floor beside her desk. We watched the mouse inch towards it with its tiny little feet, silently making its way across the floor. The mouse crawled up the wide strap of her purse and dropped from view. Velma put her hand in the air, torn between being yelled at for disturbing the class, and worried about the consequences of keeping quiet. "Please Miss, there is a mouse in your purse," she said meekly. Miss Crosby froze on the spot.

Cecil was out of his desk in a split second. He rushed to the desk, grabbed the purse, and made a beeline for the back door. He upended the purse, and everything Miss Crosby owned flew in every direction. I was sure Velma and Cecil were really in for it for causing such a commotion, but Miss Crosby, white as a sheet, overlooked the outburst and, in fact, seemed grateful.

The next morning, she arrived at the school with a brown bag from Briscoe's General Store. Ordering Cecil and Emerson up to her desk, she turned the bag over and about eight mousetraps fell onto her desk. She instructed the lads to set them at every hole in the baseboards around the room.

Now it was harder than ever to concentrate. When we should have been looking at the blackboard, our eyes would slip over to the line-up of mousetraps around the wall. They started to go off about an hour after school started. Every time one snapped, our eyes flew to Miss Crosby, who sat at her desk, wincing and ramrod straight in her chair. I couldn't bear to look at the mice, and neither could the rest of the girls at the Northcote School.

It was soon obvious to all of us that Miss Crosby was going to have to think of something, and fast. By noon hour, the boys in Senior Fourth had disposed of all the mice and returned the traps to Miss Crosby. The girls were sent outside at recess and the boys were kept in school. We could hear slamming and banging around, and Joyce said it sounded like

Miss Crosby had gone mad and was beating up on every boy in the school. Finally, she emerged with the brass bell, and we girls marched inside to we knew not what, cold and shivering from the frigid day.

Our eyes flew to the baseboards. The big yardstick that hung at the front of the room had been broken into pieces, and every hole in the wall had been nailed shut. It was a makeshift job, but the boys had little to work with. We never saw another mouse that winter. Cecil hissed, as he slid in his seat behind Velma and me, that the traps were at that very minute burning away in the old oil-drum stove. Miss Crosby had once again come up with a solution to rid us of distractions and keep her purse free of any uninvited visitors.

A Bad Day in Northcote

I should have known when my feet hit the floor that morning that it was not going to be a good day. The fire had gone out through the night, and the stovepipe that snaked through our bedroom was as cold as ice. That meant that the ankles of my long underwear had not dried. I dipped them in the wash basin every night so that they would be nice and tight the next day under my long, ribbed stockings. I looked at them hanging there on the back of a chair. They looked like two dishcloths frozen to a clothesline.

The next calamity to strike was when I was making the toast over the hole in the Findlay Oval. Emerson whacked me on the back and the entire rack of toast, four full slices, slid into the stove. Mother gave Emerson a cuff on the ear that sent him reeling, which meant that I would probably get whacked even harder when Emerson got me alone.

Mother put my long underwear on the oven door and it was thawed out and almost dry by the time I was ready to dress for school. I rolled it on, put my long beige, ribbed stockings on top and then my fleece-lined, navy blue bloomers over everything. When we left the house, it was a mild winter's day. Mother said that since I had three layers on under my skirt and coat, I could probably walk to school without my snowpants. I remember thinking that was the first good thing to come my way that morning.

Since it was a nice day, Miss Crosby insisted every last one of us vacate the school at recess. I would much rather have stayed in and drawn on the blackboard, but there was nothing more final than an order from Miss Crosby.

All winter the boys of the Northcote School had been piling snow against the west fence in the yard. They carried pail after pail of water from the iron pump and sloshed it down to form a slide of ice. The boys kept a supply of big cardboard boxes at the back of the school to use for sleighs, and every recess was spent lining up for a turn to slide down the pile of snow.

The changing weather, however, had turned the boxes into sodden messes, and Cecil said we would have to get a new supply from Briscoe's General Store to replace them. There was enough ice though, he explained, to slide down without benefit of anything. So, after climbing with great effort to the crest, we lined up at the top of this mound.

The slide down took less than five seconds, but no one ever considered that the climb was hardly worth the effort. There we were, lined up like clay pigeons, waiting our turn. We would take a little run of a couple steps, slam our bottoms down on the mound, stick our feet straight out, and down we would go. We all got about five turns before Miss Crosby came to the door and rang the hand bell.

I knew I was in trouble as soon as I took off my coat. I was soaked to the skin, and silently cursed myself for not wearing my snowpants to school like every other girl there had done. Well, nothing missed that eagle eye of Miss Crosby. She immediately saw my black serge skirt sticking to my legs. After ordering me to the cloakroom, she followed me in. Miss Crosby stripped me of my underclothes and handed me a pair of big flour-bag bloomers that she kept for the pupil who was chosen to scrub the floor at the first of every month.

Surely, she didn't expect me to go into the schoolroom dressed in those, I thought. She was muttering away about not wanting to be responsible for my catching pneumonia and was herding me back out to my desk with my sodden underwear, ribbed stockings and blue bloomers in her hand. My skirt did little to conceal the enormous bloomers, and to add to my humiliation, Miss Crosby stretched my underwear and stockings over the backs of two chairs, tight to the oil-drum stove, to dry out.

My underpinnings spent the day in full view. You could see, as plain as day, where the dye had come out of the navy blue bloomers and was imbedded forever in the seat of my long drawers.

I couldn't look at Marguerite who was snickering like a sick cat. By four o'clock, everything was dry, and I went back into the cloakroom to change. My older sister Audrey was waiting to walk me home. She knew I thought it was the very worst day of my entire life. Audrey, who always tried to find a silver lining in every cloud, said it could have been worse. Nothing, I thought, could have been worse. "Oh, yes," Audrey said. "You could have been wearing your flour-bag underwear with Five Roses stencilled across the back."

The Last Day

oday, the last day of school means simply that studies are over. The children and the teachers leave the classrooms, the custodians take over to clean out the last traces of the year's wear and tear, and the building is rarely given another thought until September.

Back in the thirties, when I was growing up on a Renfrew County farm, closing the school for the summer was a lot of work—for the pupils and the teacher. We were rarely spared from our studies on the morning of the last day of school. Just because the school year was going to end at four o'clock, was no reason not to go over the previous day's work one more time. Miss Crosby was one of those old-time teachers who followed, to the letter, the curriculum as was set down by the Department of Education. Never let it be said that her pupils were caught slacking, even if it was the last day of school.

After eating our lunches outside that day, we had to formally line up when Miss Crosby rang the big brass bell from the front step, just like any other time of the year. The first thing to catch our eye on going into the schoolhouse, was the neat pile of white foolscap sheets at the right-hand corner of Miss Crosby's desk, right beside the bible and the big black dictionary. The sheets hadn't been there in the morning, and we knew we wouldn't be handed them until minutes before school was dismissed at four o'clock that day. That pile of papers sent a chill over the room that even a hot June afternoon couldn't dispel. These were the final exams we had laboured over the week before. Right beside them were the report cards, face down so that no one could accidentally read them. They were to be handed out with our marked exams.

Before we were allowed to know our fate for the coming year, we had a major chore to do. That routine of the last day never varied as long as I went to the Northcote School. We, the pupils, were expected to clean the entire schoolhouse from top to bottom, so that it would be ready for our return two months later.

Miss Crosby would make a list of everyone's individual responsibilities, and this, too, was not brought out of her desk until after the lunch hour. The list included things like washing the windows inside and out, scrubbing the blackboards, cleaning out the desks, washing the desktops and burning the trash in a big oil drum in the backyard. To a couple of the pupils in Senior Fourth, went the job of scrubbing the wood floor until it glistened. The potbellied stove would have to have its ashes carried out to the back fence, and the pipe with the damper in it would be stuffed with scrunched-up newspaper, so that any birds planning on nesting in the chimney over the summer couldn't find their way into the school. Oh, Miss Crosby thought of everything.

When the chores were done, and we had all taken our seats once again, she would examine in minute detail the entire classroom, rubbing her hands over the window ledges, and peeking under lifted desktops. Heaven help the pupil who didn't do a job to her liking!

During the inspection, we sat ramrod straight, somehow thinking that if we were on our very best behaviour, those frightening sheets of paper and the report cards would have nothing but high marks and praises written on them. Finally, Miss Crosby would glide to the front of the classroom (she never walked anywhere), and I always thought her face softened a bit at that point.

She had the report cards arranged so that they corresponded with the pile of exams. As she took one in her hand, she tucked the proper number of exams into the centre of the card. She called each pupil by name, starting with the youngest. Each of us, in turn, left our seat, went up to her desk and accepted the pile from her hand. Formally, she shook hands with each of us, and then we trembled all the way back to our desks. Never a word was spoken, but we did glance at those who had already made the pilgrimage to the teacher's desk, and one look would tell us if it was good or bad news that greeted each pupil.

When that task was finished, Miss Crosby would glide to the door and announce that school was dismissed, and that she hoped we would have a good, productive summer. That meant, of course, that she expected us to keep our schoolwork in mind. Then she would say that, with the exception of the entrance class, she would see all of us back in September.

Only when I was safely on the road home from the Northcote School would I venture a look at the report card. Today, I can still see that beautiful clear penmanship of a favourite teacher, and in my mind I can picture those magic words: Mary Haneman, promoted to Junior Third. Only then could I really appreciate that school was out, and stretched before me were two glorious, carefree months.

Neighbours

A good neighbour was as essential to our survival in the thirties as was a good crop of grain…or a sudden rain in a season of drought. Without neighbours, each one looking out for the other, the Depression would have been unbearable. Our very existence depended on the hand of friendship from a neighbour who was attuned to the needs of those around him and who, without being asked, was there when he was needed most. This was the creed of the Depression. It seems to me now, so many years later, that our lives were so intertwined with those of our neighbours that they were like a loving family.

"Thrashings" (it was only years later that I learned that the proper word was "threshings") were community affairs. Whoever had the threshing machine went from farm to farm, followed by neighbours from miles around. They would arrive by horse and buggy, battered old trucks, or on foot, and by the end of the day the grain was bagged and ready for the barn. At noon hour the men would come for dinner (supper was at night and lunch was the snack you had before you went to bed). They would wash up in the communal basin that sat on a bench just inside the kitchen door, and dry their calloused hands on the huck roller towel before heading for the table.

The woman of the house, often given a hand by a neighbour, would have worked well into the night to be ready for the next day. Fresh bread, pies cut in four and bowls of homemade pickles would already be on the table when the men came in. Mounds of steaming hot potatoes, carrots and turnips, and a pitcher full to the brim of gravy to go with the haunch of beef, would vanish before your very eyes. It was the woman's job to keep the bowls full and the bread plate heaping.

This respite from the threshing would be nothing more than a pause in the workday. When the white granite teapot, which had been boiling on the back of the cookstove, came to the oilcloth-covered table, the men poured their own. The pie plates would be emptied as fast as the woman of the house could replenish them, with some of the neighbours devouring two or three pieces while they chatted and blew on their cups full of steaming green tea. Then it was back to the job at hand, and the next day and the ones after that would find the same neighbours doing the same thing until the entire community had been covered.

Barn raisings were done in the same fashion. If a fire destroyed a farmer's barns, he knew that as soon as the last flicker of flame was gone, a contingent of neighbours would move in after doing up their own chores. They would clean up the debris, lumber would be hauled from the mill (and of course, "put on the bill until the beef sale"), and within days a new barn would have risen from the ashes.

Neighbours traded, bartered and borrowed. Usually, little or no money changed hands.

When it came time to rest at the end of the workweek, neighbours met at the homesteads for what were known as the Saturday-night parties. Since most of the homes were without electricity, coal-oil lamps filled every downstairs window, but on Saturday night, the Coleman lamp was lit. The little sack which produced the light on the Coleman lanterns was an expensive luxury, so was only used on company evenings and special occasions.

You didn't need a formal invitation to show up at the Saturday-night house party, you just showed up. Off in a corner of the parlour, some of the guests played six-hand euchre at a makeshift table. In our house, an old slab pine door rested on the backs of four chairs for this purpose. All the kitchen furniture would be moved to the sides to clear the floor for the square dance.

There was always someone who could play the spoons (it was often my Father, who couldn't carry a tune in a pail, but had a good sense of rhythm), Uncle Alec (not an uncle at all, but we always thought he could have been) arrived with his homemade fiddle, and the men would take turns calling for the squares.

The old Findlay Oval would be crackling and spewing out heat, but the dancers wouldn't stop for a break until the perspiration poured down their faces. The music would continue, with the spoons and the fiddle changing from breakdown music to a different beat. Some of the men, and occasionally a woman or two, would go to the centre of the kitchen and stomp out a kind of two-step jig that had us all clapping our hands and pounding our feet to the rhythm.

Then there was the lunch. Always there was a lunch. Ample and home-made, with eleven-quart baskets of sandwiches with their crusts left on, the inevitable pots of green tea and big slab cakes. This was when the neighbours sat around the kitchen and the parlour and talked about the Depression…and the farmer who was sick and not able to tend his stock… Plans would be made to help out whoever was in need. They talked about the rumours of war, and about farm loans, and if there was enough hay in the loft to tide them over the winter.

Almost as predictable as the Saturday-night house party was Sunday church. Although most communities had a mix of different religions and beliefs, church played a paramount role. If there were religious tensions, we as children were not aware of them. What we were aware of was the philosophy that it mattered not *what* church you went to, but it mattered that you went to church.

It was a combination of the friendly and willing help in times of need, the companionship and the strong faith, that held the neighbours together. I know for a fact that the community I grew up in was not unique for the times. Pockets of neighbours all over held the same strong feelings of commitment to each other. You see, the Depression knew no bounds. It didn't just happen in Renfrew County, or on the Prairies, or in the rolling hills of Kentucky. The Depression was universal. That is why I think those who survived the Depression were a special breed of people. The legacy they left us is one of resilience and perseverance, commitment to helping a neighbour and, of course, pride in a job well done. What better heritage could we ask for?

Neighbourly Cures

Mrs. Beam was a wonderful old German neighbour we called on in times of grave illnesses, births and any ailment that went on longer than a few days. Her cures usually worked, but alas, the patient lived in mortal dread that unless he shaped up in a hurry, the woman with the poker-straight silver hair and enormous girth would be descending on the house and taking over. Unless Mrs. Beam declared the cure beyond her capabilities, and death was just around the corner, old Doctor Murphy from town was never consulted.

During late winter each year, it seemed that everyone in our house came down with what was commonly known as the grip. To me that always meant a great, racking cough, a sore throat and a stomach ache. Mrs. Beam would be summoned and I would be handed over to her care like a lamb about to be given up for sacrifice.

Her tamer cures involved a dirty wool sock wrapped around the sore throat, and a hateful mixture of onion, coal oil and honey, which we had to sip from a hot spoon. I have no idea if the passing of time or the concoction was the cure, but I confess it worked.

Sometimes, when I was sick with the grip, I wouldn't tell Mrs. Beam if I also had a sick stomach. The treatment for that used to have me in tears at the very thought. She would lead us upstairs where the banister circled the stairwell. Then she would bend us over the banister with our tummies hard against the rail. Next, she would give us a slap on the back with her slat of a hand that would knock the wind out of us. Fortunately, she had a good hold of our underwear or we would have gone headlong down the stairwell.

Now, I had no idea if it was this cruel treatment that got rid of the stomach ache or the sheer terror of being whacked again, but it always cured me instantly. Why we didn't suffer permanent injury is beyond me to this day.

Mrs. Beam always said if you wanted to beat a cold at its own game you had to eat an enormous breakfast. She explained that all her treatments were for naught unless you downed a heaping bowl of porridge, eggs, potatoes, fried pork and at least two slices of thick toast. To her credit, she had the good sense not to try the banister treatment right after we had eaten breakfast.

Mrs. Beam always thought that treating any illness was part old-fashioned remedy, and part folklore. When she was summoned to our house, she would first administer her treatments and then leave a series of explicit (and often absurd) instructions for us to follow. She said the treatment was useless without following the customs her great grand-mother had brought over from Germany. Many of them made absolutely no sense to me whatsoever, but we so lived in dread of the consequences of not doing exactly what we were told, that we five children followed her instructions to the letter.

For instance, Mrs. Beam said you never, ever got out of the side of the bed when you had the grip. You must crawl over the foot. Now that was quite a task with the old iron beds we had back in the thirties. I can still picture my sister Audrey and I coughing and gasping for breath, crawling to the foot of our beds in the morning and heaving ourselves over the iron frame. You wouldn't dare think to ask Mrs. Beam what the exercise had to do with the curing of the grip. If you did so, she would shoot you a despicable look that hushed you up in a hurry and had you hanging your head in shame for questioning her.

I would like to tell you what Mrs. Beam recommended for the runs, but the memory—although vivid in my mind—is too painful to recall. Let it suffice to say that the very thought of it sends cramps careening through my lower regions like an electric shock.

Today, the drugstore shelves are filled with over-the-counter cures for every ailment imaginable. Some work, and some don't, and some cost a month's rent! I will say this for old Mrs. Beam, her treatments worked. They were certainly a test of one's endurance, but if she said you would be up and running in two days, that's exactly when you could count on being on your feet again. Her visits also served the purpose of having a neighbourly visit with Mother, who craved company. The biggest bonus of all, however, was that Mrs. Beam's advice was free. Back in those Depression years, that was the biggest reward of all.

One Good Deed Deserves Another

The little dog I called Blondie filled my heart with joy. I was only about five when I got her, and I loved her passionately. She was just a bundle of golden fluff, certainly not the kind of dog that served much use on a farm. She couldn't even bark very loud, so she could never be considered a watchdog. I was sure she would protect me from any danger to come my way, and on more than one occasion I vowed I would gladly die for her.

To this end, one of the blackest days of my life was the day she caught her leg in a swinging barn door and broke it. It didn't help at all when Emerson reminded me that she would probably go the way of all injured farm animals and be "put out of her misery," as it was called. I was so frantic with grief that I carried Blondie into the kitchen and begged my mother to do something. The leg hung down like a rag, and the little dog whimpered softly in my arms. It was then, in my blackest hour, that I thought of our neighbour, Mrs. Beam. Didn't she deliver babies and cure pneumonia…and get rid of boils…and have magic potions which she administered for every ailment from the flu to head lice? I begged my mother to let me phone Mrs. Beam. I'm not sure if it was sympathy for Blondie, or concern for her sobbing child, but Mother agreed I could call our neighbour for advice. "But if she says nothing can be done, then you have to accept what that means," Mother warned. Only too well did I know what it meant!

Without even telling Mrs. Beam what I wanted her for, I cried into the phone that I had to see her right away. I was not the least surprised when she said she would be right over. It was only a few minutes until I saw her horse and buggy pull into the yard.

Mrs. Beam always carried her remedies in an old, brown leather suitcase which had seen better days. She flopped it up onto the kitchen table and asked Mother who was ailing. "Its Blondie," I wailed. "She has a broken leg." I begged her to fix it and reminded her what the consequences were if she couldn't. I was still holding my dog in my arms, and Mrs. Beam took her and gently laid her on the kitchen table. This, of course, didn't please Mother one bit, since she felt all animals belonged in the barn. Never in her entire life would she ever let me put my dog up on the kitchen table.

She looked at the broken leg for a long time. Then she went to the woodbox and got a small piece of kindling. Without as much as a by-your-leave, she opened the kitchen drawer and took out the butcher knife. With one whack, she split the kindling into fragments, sending pieces flying in every direction.

She then went to the rag bag (every kitchen in Renfrew County had a rag bag), took out a piece of cotton and tore it into strips. She told me to hold the broken leg gently, and she made a splint and attached it to Blondie's broken leg. When the leg was secure to her satisfaction, she opened a bottle of brown liquid, which looked suspiciously like the same medicine she gave us for the whooping cough, and poured some of it down Blondie's throat. Without wiping the neck of the bottle, she capped it and put it back in her bag, ready for the next patient. I could see Mother flinch.

Mrs. Beam said Blondie would sleep the rest of the day, and that the splint was to stay on for several weeks. She told me that in no time the dog would be as right as rain. I put my pet behind the kitchen stove on an old blanket, and watched her doze off almost immediately.

I was so grateful to Mrs. Beam that I ran upstairs to my washstand to bring down whatever money I had tied in the corner of my hanky.

I suddenly remembered I had spent it on penny candy at Briscoe's General Store, so I reached into my drawer and took out my most prized possession. It was a bottle of Lily of the Valley perfume Aunt Lizzie had given me.

I pressed it into Mrs. Beam's hand and told her it was in payment of fixing Blondie's leg. She looked at the perfume for a long time, and then she handed it back to me. She said that was what neighbours were for—doing good turns for one another—and if I really wanted to pay her I could do a favour for someone else. That's the way things were done in the thirties…that's how we all survived.

Old Herman on the Line

Old Herman held out from getting a telephone installed until he was shamed into it. He lived on a farm surrounded by neighbours who had finally relented and given in to this newfangled invention, but he saw no reason why he should put out that kind of money if it wasn't necessary.

Now, Old Herman, being a bachelor, probably had more money than all the farmers on the side road combined. He spent little, wore clothes that were in ribbons, and always managed to get several good meals a week just by happening to drop into someone's kitchen as a hearty supper was being dished up. He had an old truck, but it never went much farther than Briscoe's General Store.

On one of his supper stopovers, the subject of the telephone came up again. He had used our phone (which had been installed courtesy of a generous donation from Uncle Lou in New York). Father emphasized to him again that it had been put in at great expense, and for our own use. Old Herman seemed to miss the point entirely and proceeded to make a few calls since, as he reasoned, he was going to be there for a few hours anyway. His brother lived down the road, and a few nieces and nephews farmed in the area as well. When he finished his calls, he repeated that he could see no reason to have a phone when he had such good neighbours all around him who had this new contraption.

I could see Father was losing his patience. "Now see here, Herman, you're just bein' plain miserable. There is no earthly reason why you shouldn't have a phone. You live alone back in the bush, and you never know when you'll need something in a hurry." Old Herman squirmed on his chair and chewed his wad of tobacco faster than I had ever seen him chew before. Father kept up the attack.

Finally, Old Herman admitted he never liked the thought of his house being wired up to a pole with all that electricity. He was just plain scared to take the chance that all those wires might start on fire some night when he was asleep in his bed, and then where would he be? Back in Rosemount Cemetery, that's where! Father knew there was no sense in explaining to Old Herman that electricity had nothing to do with it. We had a phone but no electricity.

Mother now cut into the conversation. She told Old Herman that his reasoning and fears were sheer nonsense and that he was just a stubborn old German who refused to accept new ways. Mother also continued that he was the talk of the township because he was the only one on the Northcote Side Road who didn't have a phone. After Mother's outburst, Herman slammed down his fist on the table and boomed, "All right. I'll have the dashed thing put in, but if something happens to me or my house, you'll be responsible!" Mother dished him up another piece of apple pie, and patted him on the shoulder in maternal fashion.

I'll say one thing for Old Herman, if he said he was going to do something, he did it! About a week later, as we five kids were racing home from the Northcote School to beat a storm that was brewing in the west, we saw that the telephone lines were attached to poles in Old Herman's lane. By the time we hit the yard, the rain was starting and the thunder was cracking all around us. I was terrified of storms, so I headed right for the house to hide under the feather tickings in my bed, as I always did.

At the height of the storm, our phone rang—two longs and a short. Father lifted off the receiver, and we heard him say "hello" to Old Herman. We never did know what happened next, but Father dropped the receiver and it dangled on its long wire against the wall. Father kept yelling into the mouthpiece, "Herman, are you there?" It was soon obvious that the connection was broken. "Probably the storm," I heard Father say as I slid deeper under the tickings.

It wasn't long before we saw Old Herman's truck drive into the yard. The storm had abated, and now it was just a heavy rain. Old Herman was fuming. His feet barely touched the ground, and he didn't even bother to knock. "You and that darn newfangled contraption! Just look what it did to my ear. It nearly killed me, that's what!"

We all rushed over to where Old Herman was standing, dripping wet, at the back door. Mother peered at the ear in question. It certainly looked red, she admitted. Then the story came out. Old Herman had just had the phone wired up that afternoon and thought he'd make a few calls before his supper. Nobody told him not to use the dashed thing in a storm! A bolt of lightning that, according to Old Herman, shook the rafters of the house, followed the wires right into the receiver. He claimed the sparks burnt his ear. He was so mad that he fixed that phone good! He ripped the thing right off the wall, and there it would stay until someone from the office in Renfrew came to pick it up! If Mother wouldn't mind calling them in the morning, and telling them to take it off his property, he would be much obliged. Audrey was already setting another place at the table, and Mother said as far as she was concerned, the ear looked fine to her.

All through supper, the storm seemed to come and go. With every bolt of lightning, our phone would give out little pings of protest. Each time, Old Herman would lift his eyes from his heaping plate and give the machine a look of pure hatred.

Hallowe'en

Hallowe'en was supposed to be a fun night, but for me, unless I could cling tightly to my older sister Audrey's hand, I went to the yearly party with a mixture of anticipation and plain fear. That year was to be no different.

The school, the church basement, a neighbour's home or big barn was usually chosen as the meeting place and we all descended on the spot for one big and glorious Hallowe'en party. That was the night the spirits of our ancestors came out, old Granny Hines rode across the black sky on her broom, and ghosts hovered behind every shrub. At least that's what we younger children firmly believed. Is it any wonder I stuck to my sister Audrey like flypaper all evening?

One year I remember above all others. It was mild for the end of October, "almost like summer," Father had said as we all piled into the old Model T to be driven over to Croziers' barn. Emerson, of course, immediately set about scaring the daylights out of me, declaring he saw great-grandfather Haneman at the mailbox, shaking his fist in our direction. "Looked just like his picture hanging in the parlour," he said. I burrowed my face into Audrey's shoulder. Emerson tried to twist my face into the black night, but I wouldn't budge. Suddenly, there was the most ungodly bang…just like an explosion. Emerson jumped into the front seat beside Father before any of us had a chance to scream. I heard Father say a few choice swear words in German, and the bump, bump of the car told us we had blown a tire.

Everett was the only one who would get out of the car to hold the lantern while Father made the change. Father was well prepared. Flat tires were as regular as clockwork.

We could hear Father and Everett muttering behind the car, and the very next thing we heard was someone banging on the hood. With no headlights, it was impossible to see what was causing all the commotion. I peeked out from my hiding place into the darkness and saw a black face looking in the side of the car. He held up a lantern, gave a toothless grin and—in a voice as hard as nails—said he was a spirit from ages past. Well, I never saw anyone vacate a car as fast as Emerson. He didn't even stop to open the door of the old Model T. He jumped right out the front window and never even touched the running board. He went screaming around to the back of the car, and from the sound of things, he tackled Father at full speed. I don't think I took a breath all the time the creature stood there. When he saw that he had petrified us beyond redemption, he took off his hat, popped his false teeth into his mouth, and at once we recognized Uncle Alec, our next-door neighbour.

He was slapping his leg and laughing his head off. Emerson crawled back into the car and said he knew it was Uncle Alec all the time. Uncle Alec crawled into the front seat with Father, and they both had a good laugh as we continued on our way over to the Crozier farm.

When Father saw that the gate into their lane was closed, he asked one of the brothers to jump out and open it. Earl, the youngest, said he was sleeping in the back seat. Everett said he had helped change the tire. Emerson, lacking an excuse, was propelled out of the car by Father.

Well, the fun had only begun. Hiding at the gate were two visions that looked remarkably like ghosts. They made a leap at Emerson just as he reached for the gate. Even in the dim lights of the lamps on the car, we could see the terror on his face. He landed on the hood of the car with the two white apparitions right behind him. Father pulled him in by the seat of his pants, and said, "Boy that was close, they almost got you."

It was Uncle Alec who got out to open the gate and chase away the white figures. Finally, after what seemed like hours, we drove into the Crozier barnyard. Lanterns hung from the gateposts, and we could hear the fiddle music coming from the barn. Emerson was the first to go through the doorway. He looked as calm as a cucumber as he sauntered over to where the boys from the Northcote School were hanging out. He certainly didn't look like the young boy who was scared half out of his wits a few minutes ago. "It's amazing what a few lights will do," Father said to Uncle Alec.

Dead Air

*I*t had been a wet, snowy day and now the snow had turned to ice pellets. Father said it was a perfect night to sit in by the raging Findlay Oval with his feet up on the oven door, and with the *Family Herald* and *Weekly Star* beside his chair. The rest of the family, after my sister Audrey and I had redded up the kitchen, were trying to settle down to those activities which kept us busy on a Saturday night.

The phone rang—two longs and a short. Emerson raced to the oak apparatus, which hung on the wall by the back door and yelled hello into the mouthpiece. It was for Mother. "Wonder who could be calling at this hour of the night," she said. It seemed to be a one-way conversation. Finally Mother said. "I think that would be lovely. We'll be right over."

Whatever invitation she had accepted, Father wasn't consulted. I could see his face cloud over as he saw his quiet evening at home in a warm kitchen fade before his eyes.

Mother said it was Uncle Alec Thom on the next farm. "You know that radio the Thoms bought before Christmas. Well, Alec finally figured out how it works, and we are all invited over for the evening to listen to it."

With the exception of Father, none of us could contain our excitement. We were in our warm clothes in a flash, and Mother finally talked Father into doing the neighbourly thing and joining us, so that Uncle Alec's feelings wouldn't be hurt. I heard him wonder aloud if anyone cared about *his* feelings.

We had to take the sleigh because the path between the two farms was nothing but glare ice. Even though the weather was frightful, not much time had passed between the phone call and when we slid up to the Thoms' door.

When we got our outer clothes off, we could see Aunt Bertha had arranged the chairs in a semicircle around the small table by her sewing machine. The room looked a lot like the O'Brien Theatre in Renfrew. We all took seats, and Aunt Bertha turned off all the lights except the one at the back door. The Thoms had got electricity the year before. Apart from the radio, that had put them a cut above the Haneman family, I thought.

Uncle Alec had placed his chair in front of the brown box, which was the radio. It had several dials on the front, and a piece of knubby material stretched over a cut-out circle in the middle. It was an awesome sight, all right!

Then the most awful squawking we had ever heard came out of it. "Turn it down," Aunt Bertha yelled above the din. Uncle Alec fooled with the knobs and all we could hear was a noise like someone scratching chalk on a blackboard, only twice as loud. He assured us it would soon come through loud and clear. Unfortunately, nothing he could do with the knobs seemed to get rid of the static. Finally, we heard a man say, "Chicago," and then the noise took over again. Emerson started to laugh. Mother poked him from behind with the toe of her shoe.

Uncle Alec unplugged and plugged it in again to the same socket. It made no difference. Other than the odd word here and there, we couldn't make out any of the dialogue that came out of the top of the radio where the speaker was.

Ralph, the oldest of the Thom boys, said he might be able to do something with it. He said he had sat in Briscoe's General Store only last week and listened to their radio. Uncle Alec invited him to try. The room was hushed again. Ralph turned one knob and then the other. The static was even louder than before. He gave it a slap on the side, and the thing died altogether. Uncle Alec raced to the plug in the wall and did exactly what he had done before. The fearful noises came back loud and clear. Aunt Bertha said she was very disappointed because Major Bowes' *Amateur*

Hour was supposed to be on, and even if Uncle Alec got the thing working, the program would be half over. My little friend Velma and I were playing shadows on the wall with our hands or we would have been bored beyond belief.

After a good hour, it was apparent to even the youngest of us that there was going to be no radio at the Thoms that night. Aunt Bertha said maybe we should give it a rest and she would make a cup of tea. It seems to me now that a cup of tea was the cure for just about anything back in the thirties.

One more try later failed to muster more than a squawk from the radio. As she bundled us into our coats, Mother said that it had been a nice outing anyway. We climbed onto the flat-bottomed sleigh and headed across the field. Hardly a word was spoken. Once we were all back in the house, Father, with his eyes squinted as if trying to see into the future, said in his best 'I told you so' voice, "You know those radios? I don't think they'll ever catch on."

The New Choir Member

Mother said he was the most unsavoury character she had ever met. For once, Father didn't argue. Even though the farmer was a neighbour, whom Father had met on many an occasion, Mother saw to it that there was nothing sociable about their encounters.

First of all, as far as she was concerned, he was too fond of the drink. He not only indulged in homemade brew, whose very origin seemed to qualify it as an unacceptable beverage, but it was the bottles he bought in Renfrew when his children were denied the bare necessities of life, that upset Mother.

Father said that was an exaggeration. At any rate, we all knew this neighbour had earned what old Granny Hines called "a reputation that would please the devil."

That all changed one weekend when we went to the Lutheran Church and there he was, sitting right up in the choir loft with a look of utter piety on his face. Father said he probably had received a higher calling. Emerson wondered if he had seen a vision or something like that. Mother hissed that the only vision he ever saw was through the neck of a bottle.

Father said it was our duty to accept that the man had changed, and rejoice in his new-found piety. And every Sunday thereafter, the man, dressed in his best suit, sat up in the choir belting out the hymns. The organist seemed delighted as there weren't too many men from the farming community who wanted to sing in the choir. After a while it looked like the man had always been there. Mother, being a good friend of the man's wife, said she was a saint...plain and simple...a real saint, to live with a man like that. She felt that nobody should condemn her just because she had made a bad choice for a husband.

One evening Mother had occasion to go over to the farm in question. I was allowed to go too, since I had all my chores done, and my hateful brother Emerson had teased me to the point of tears at the supper table.

As it turned out, that was the same evening the organist held choir practice. It was with more than a little bit of pride that the wife of the new choir member relayed this message to Mother. "That's where he is...down at the Lutheran Church practising the hymns for Sunday," she said.

It was pitch-black when we struck out for home in the old Model T. We were coming up the Northcote Side Road, picking our way along the familiar landmarks, when we heard the bang. Without a word between us, we knew exactly what it was...another flat tire!

Mother said there was no way she was going to try to replace it in the dark. It was just a few yards down the road to Old Herman's and she would ask him to drive us home in the horse and buggy. I clutched Mother's hand, and with the lantern we always carried for just such an emergency, we started walking.

Now, Old Herman never went to church. He swore like a sailor, and Mother said he wore the same suit of long underwear from the first snowfall to the spring runoff. How she knew this was beyond me. At any rate, we headed into Herman's lane, following the small glow of a coal-oil lamp in his window. We fumbled our way up the back steps, in through the summer kitchen, and tapped on the door.

Herman swung it wide open, revealing a smoke-filled kitchen and a small group of men sitting around the kitchen table. They were hot in the middle of a wild poker game. Piles of coins and a few bills were in the middle of the table, and low and behold, there sat our newly acclaimed choir member. His fist was full of cards and he had a look on his face that defied description.

Mother glared him down. "And when do you start singing hymns?" she asked him pointedly. There was no answer.

When Old Herman heard our plight, he shooed us out the door to the drive shed. Not a word was said about the poker game all the way home.

When Father heard the story, he tried to justify the neighbour's behaviour by saying that using choir practice as an excuse was probably the only way the poor man could get out of the house. Mother wasn't buying that story.

The next Sunday, the chair belonging to the erstwhile choir member sat empty. Father said at least he gave the man credit for not adding "hypocrite" to his list of sins.

The Witch of Northcote

I wasn't exactly overjoyed at going over to Granny Hines' old, black log house across our back field. We called it Granny Hines' house, even though she didn't own it. She lived there with her son, daughter-in-law and five granddaughters. I knew perfectly well she was a witch, and unless I was well-fortified by several brothers and a sister, I preferred to stay well clear of the place. Especially when I knew no one was home but Granny Hines.

That Saturday, Mother was having no part of my objections. Granny Hines loved Mother's sticky buns, and a fresh batch had just come out of the oven. I was dispatched across the field with the brown paper bag in hand. I was especially leery because I had seen the family go out the lane with the horse and driving buggy a short while before. They were no doubt headed to Renfrew for the week's supplies. I counted heads and knew perfectly well that everyone was gone except old Granny Hines. I also knew I would be in for a session of Granny's ghost stories, which I tingled over if my older sister and brothers were around but had no intention of listening to if I was the only one there.

I delayed the trip across the field as long as I could. I changed my clothes and took a long time in the privy, but eventually I had to face the music. I headed across the field to the old log house that beckoned me as sure as if it crooked a finger in my direction. I kept turning around to look at our own home. It was log too, but to me it wasn't nearly as menacing.

When I reached the point where I could no longer see my mother in the garden, I really started to shake and tremble. It was a small wooded area, not more than a few hundred feet thick, but nonetheless my mind always whirled to the story of *Little Red Riding Hood*, which is one fable I could easily have done without.

I could hear a rustling in the trees. I stopped dead in my tracks. I knew without hesitation it was a wolf. When the black apparition appeared, it was none other than Granny Hines picking her way in my direction. As always, she was dressed completely in black, except for the starched white pinny she wore on the top of everything.

I thrust the buns in her direction. "Mother sent these. And I better be off home before it gets dark," I stuttered. Granny Hines was going to have none of that. She said it was too hard for her to carry the sack and manage her walking stick at the same time. I was to go with her to the menacing little house.

There was nothing I could do but do as I was bid. I never took my eyes off the old woman who kept up a steady chatter about the dangers of walking through the bush alone. This did little to calm my racing heart, knowing I would be making the return trip alone.

Granny Hines had old ears. The lobes were pleated and long and hung down her neck like bowls on a teaspoon. I could see them wobble as she walked, which helped take my mind off my mission. When we were only a few yards from the clearing, her old log house came into view. I made up my mind then and there that under no condition would I darken the door.

Granny Hines was talking about all the tramps walking the tracks those days. Said one came right up to the house only the week before. A person wasn't safe anywhere. Important to keep the house locked up when you were out, even if it was just at neighbours'. My eyes scanned the yard looking for a tramp. With great effort, Granny Hines climbed the three steps to the back door. There was a nail stuck in the doorframe on which, in plain view, hung a big long key. She reached up and pulled the key off the nail and unlocked the back door.

I wanted to ask her about the merits of locking a door and then leaving the key where everyone could see it, but thought better of prolonging the visit. I thrust the bag of still-warm buns in her direction. She asked me to come in and sit for a spell...get out of the hot sun...maybe have a sip of milk. None of those offers appealed to me. She held up a big penny, which she offered me for bringing the sticky buns. I knew Mother would never approve of my taking money for a neighbourly act, so I declined, backing up all the while towards the gate leading to the trail home.

When I got to the edge of the bush, I stopped to catch my breath and prepare myself for the fast run that would take me to the clearing on the other side. I thrust my hands into my middy pockets. To my surprise, in the bottom of the right-hand pocket was something smooth like a button. I took it out and there in my hand was a penny.

To this day I have no idea how it got there. It looked exactly like the penny Granny Hines held up at the door to her old log house. I knew I hadn't taken it from her. The thought of throwing it away became paramount, because at once I knew it had been spirited into my pocket. Then I thought of the butterscotch sucker it would buy at Briscoe's General Store. I dropped the penny back inside my middy and ran through the bush like the wind, convinced more than ever that I had just had a confrontation with a real live witch.

A Fair Trade

Bartering was a way of life. Often little money changed hands. To me, there always seemed to be a constant chain of trading, swapping, and sharing workloads with a neighbour. It was a means of survival back in the thirties.

I remember a deal that was once made over a choir gown. The neighbour arrived to say that she was to be in charge of the Christmas concert that year, and I was needed in the choir. That honour, however, necessitated my having to wear a choir gown, which naturally I didn't own. The neighbour, a kindly soul, told Mother not to fret over it, as she had enough broadcloth left from making a choir gown for her daughter and she would make one for me. Mother had no money to pay for the choir gown, and so she refused the neighbour's kindly offer, much to my great disappointment.

However, we underestimated the neighbour's kind heart, and the very next Saturday, she arrived at our home with the finished gown. I was ecstatic and immediately slipped it on over my clothes.

Mother ordered me to take it off. "I have no money to pay for the broadcloth, and so Mary cannot keep it," she said with a catch in her voice. I begged, I cried, but to no avail. The gown had to be taken off.

Our neighbour told Mother how often she had offered a helping hand, and the gown would just be a small repayment. Mother would not hear of it. The gown had to be given back. With tears flowing, I took off the gown.

Then the neighbour did something that was truly indicative of the times. She started towards the door, refusing to take back the gown, which Mother was folding on the table to be returned to the maker. The neighbour had got as far as opening the door a crack, when Mother called her back. "I have no money for the broadcloth. But I must give you something for it. Here is my butter dish. Please take it in payment."

Many, many years later, as this kindly neighbour was lying on her deathbed, she thought of the episode in that old log house and she called her daughter to her side. Her instructions were simple. "I owe a debt. I know Mrs. Haneman is long gone, but her daughter Mary is living, and this butter dish really belongs to her. When I am gone, you will see that she gets her mother's butter dish back."

After much searching, the daughter found me, and the blue and orange butter dish, so reminiscent of the thirties, came back. I remember how those dishes came in large bags of puffed wheat. Most of what we called "better-than-everyday dishes" were made up of these hodgepodge of cups and saucers, cereal bowls and little milk jugs, all coming as "prizes" in bags of cereal. They were cheap, made-in-China dishes with no value. To a kindly neighbour and a mother who couldn't bear to owe a debt, the butter dish, bartered for the making of a child's choir gown, has come back to its owner. It remains a prized possession and a precious reminder of the integrity of those people of the Depression years.

Stuff

For years, all the time my children were little, we always referred to the little drawer next to the kitchen sink as the miscellaneous drawer. When I went through what my family likes to call my 'reorganization and efficiency stage' in life, I wanted to put small labels on the inside edge of all my kitchen drawers so that everyone would know exactly what belonged in each. In truth, this had more to do with the lack of drawer space than with the desire to organized or efficient.

Be that as it may, when I came to labelling the miscellaneous drawer, the thirteen-letter word wouldn't fit on the label, so I decided to just write "stuff" on it instead. As a matter of fact, "stuff" described its contents perfectly.

This drawer was full of stuff. Sometimes there was so much stuff in it, that it wouldn't close, and more than once we had to slip a long steel spatula into the top of the opening to release whatever stuff was holding the drawer tight. In it there were bits and pieces of string, extra rubber rings for my blender, ties for garbage bags, kitchen scissors, half-used tubes of Crazy Glue, shoehorns, stubs of burnt candles, and so many books of paper matches that one day I tossed the whole lot of them into the fireplace! Yes, "stuff" suited the little drawer perfectly.

Then one day, a couple of years ago, I was asked to speak to a conference of Dutch Reform Church Women. I sat through long reports, some hand-clapping hymn singing, and accolades being offered to the most hardworking members. I figured most them were hardworking, because just about all of them were singled out for mention. I guessed it had something to do with the fear of committing the error of omission.

I was second-last on the program. It was a hot summer day (second only to the warmth extended to me by those in attendance) and the church, spanking new I thought, didn't have a tree in sight to offer even a bit of shade to the building. I decided that as soon as my speech was over, I would leave as unobtrusively as I could. After all, all that was left on the program was something called "entertainment." I knew that could mean anything from a "kitchen band" to someone leading a singsong.

I might have known there is nothing unobtrusive about leaving a church full of women when you are sitting in the front pew, and I realized it would be a severe breach of etiquette to get up and walk out just as we were about to be entertained. It was either divine intervention or a stroke of good luck that my exit was aborted, because part of the entertainment was the reading of a wonderful piece of wit and humour entitled "Stuff," written by Ina McElheran, a member of a local Women's Institute. Ina had given her permission to have "Stuff" read at this conference.

The piece was all about the stuff we accumulate in our lives. That included the material, the abstract, and the mental stuff that clutters our existence.

I thought about that piece for a long time. In fact, just about every day I find myself thinking about stuff. There is the stuff I have to do every day from the list I have made up the night before. This list is as important to me as doing my morning crossword puzzle. Contrary to what my husband Wally says, I can, and do, wash dishes even if that chore isn't on my list! The stuff on my daily list includes everything I have to do which could be called housework, to the deadlines I may have to meet that day. Some days the list with all the stuff on it can be as long as your arm, and then some days it may allow me a bit of leisure time. But I can tell you, there is nothing more satisfying than to cross out (in red pen, of course) each entry as I work my way down the list.

Courtesy of this list, I invariably find myself dealing with stuff I would rather avoid. Take the answering machine for instance. If I am away from my phone for any length of time, the machine will blink at me and tell me I have a message or two, or three, or more, waiting to be dealt with. I add these names to my list of stuff to do.

My house is full of stuff. Most of it I need, and if I don't, sentimentality forces me to find a place to store it. My china cabinet is full of stuff I will never use. Who uses demitasse cups today? Not me, surely; but nonetheless, I have more than a dozen of these little useless cups adding to the accumulation of stuff I have, and for which I have no use.

Stuff overflows from my filing cabinet. Someone told me when I bought my computer, I would eventually eliminate the need for my filing cabinet. If that is the case, why do I keep cramming in clippings from the newspapers, and historical data which have absolutely no significance to my work? Now, one would think with a filing cabinet overflowing with stuff, my computer would be so underutilized that I would have room for an encyclopedia and perhaps an edition of *War and Peace*. That is not necessarily the case. When I had a minor problem recently and had to call a computer expert, his first comment was, "You have an awful lot of stuff in that directory."

Then I have all this stuff you can't see. But it's there, all right. It's the stuff that is stored in my head, some of it in my subconscious and some right out in the open, but obscure enough that only I can "see" it. Here are stories not yet written. They are ideas fermenting and trying hard to develop but have yet to get beyond the dream stage.

Then there is the stuff I deal with everyday. This stuff takes precedence over everything else. It sits on the very edge of my mind, spilling over at regular intervals to remind me that I have deadlines to meet, meals to make, laundry to contend with, friends to chat with, the sick, aged and ailing to visit, letters to write, and so much other stuff of "must do" quality, that I am sometimes overwhelmed. There is no escaping this stuff. This stuff never gets on my daily list of chores. It just sits there, waiting for me to find time to squeeze it into my life.

That's what happened to the next section in this book. These stories are ones for which it would be hard to find a niche. They could loosely be called "Miscellaneous," but to me, that title didn't seem say enough, and besides, that's an awfully long word to attach to short stories. I think "Stuff" suits this section much better.

White Gloves

It always amazed me, and annoyed my brothers, that even on the hottest day in the summer, a trip into Renfrew meant the boys had to slick down their hair and put on their tweed caps. The perspiration could be pouring off the ends of their noses, but those caps had to be in place as soon as they set foot on the sidewalk.

"It's the sign of a gentleman," Mother would say. Back then, if we protested at all to our parents, it was more of a plea than a complaint. Children simply did not argue with their parents. Mother wouldn't waver. The caps stayed. They often matched the boys' breeks—grey and black, salt and pepper caps that, like as not, had come from our cousins in Regina in a hand-me-down box.

When the boys walked the streets on a Saturday night, as almost every farmer in Renfrew County did, they had to remember to immediately doff their caps when they came upon someone they knew. To do otherwise was almost as much a breach of etiquette as not wearing any cap at all. The boys would go up and down the street in a perpetual motion of donning and doffing their caps. They lamented loud and long over what they considered a silly practice, especially when they said they knew for a fact that the heads of many of the town boys never came in contact with anything remotely resembling a cap. That cut no ice with Mother. The hats stayed.

My sister Audrey and I went through the same agony over our white gloves. Happily, Mother did not make us wear our white gloves to town on Saturday night. If, however, we went to Renfrew to call on any of Mother's acquaintances, on went the silly white gloves, and on they stayed for the duration of our visit too.

As Audrey was older, her gloves had a longer cuff. I thought this gave the gloves a dashing look of elegance. Mine, however, barely covered my thumb joint. They were hateful, little, tight, white gloves that I had to struggle into on the hottest day of the summer. I wouldn't have them on two minutes when my hands would start to itch and sweat. I would sit on the edge of my chair in agony, with my hands folded in my lap as if I were having the time of my life. Heaven forbid that you would ever display anything but the happiest expression when you were in someone else's home.

It was also unheard of to go off to church without those little white gloves. There was a special routine my sister and I had to follow when we were getting ready on Sunday morning. First we had to get into our underwear and then we had to have our hair done. Then came the dresses, shoes and stockings. Finally, when we were ready to walk out the door, Mother handed us the white gloves. We were expected to carry them until we reached the churchyard, and only then were we to put them on. What a calamity it would have been to have them soiled before we walked up the aisle to our pews!

Sometimes, if we had to wear the gloves to go calling during the week, we had to be especially careful not to get them soiled. Washday was on Monday, and unlike my sister Audrey who had two pairs of gloves, I only had one. Every Sunday morning, I would examine them very carefully. I remember one time asking Mother if she thought they were clean enough to wear to church. She ripped them off my hands and said, "If you have to ask if they are dirty, then they are." I ended up wearing my sister's extra pair, miles too big but spotlessly white.

The tweed caps and the white gloves were symbols of the era. Perhaps it was a way to bring a touch of elegance or class to a time when there was no money to buy either.

Legs as Smooth as Glass

Certainly, when I was growing up, buying silk stockings wasn't an everyday occurrence. Only when the toes couldn't take another mending, and small knotted stitchings snaked up both legs, would Mother finally give in and accept that her silk stockings would have to be handed down to my sister Audrey. She would hold out as long as she could, but eventually the silk stockings would become what Mother called "indecent."

I remember the stockings well. They had silky legs with cotton heels and toes. There was a wide cotton, stretchy top and an elegant seam that ran right up the back. When it was decided that she couldn't possibly wear the old stockings one more time in public, she would have to find fifty-five cents somewhere to buy a new pair. To afford this, she either had to dip into the blue jug on the kitchen cupboard, or take another couple of chickens into town to peddle on Saturday. And when it came time for this important purchase, Mother always announced the event on the Saturday morning, writing on the top of her supply list in large print "silk stockings…Walker Stores," as if there might be some chance she would forget to pick them up.

On most Saturdays, I spent our time in Renfrew going up and down the aisles in the Five and Dime Store. But on that day, which years later became known as Silk Stocking Day, I never left Mother's side. I would suggest we could perhaps go to Walker Stores first. Mother always insisted on buying her staples first. I strongly suspect now it had something to do with seeing how much money she had left over, and if in fact there would be enough change in her little black coin purse to lay out the princely sum of fifty-five cents for a pair of stockings.

I sometimes wonder now why I was so excited about Mother buying a pair of silk stockings. After all, I wasn't getting anything new! After waiting patiently until all the other shopping was done, I could scarcely contain myself when it finally came time to go through the door of the department store. I would head right for the counter where all the boxes of stockings were stacked neatly in rows according to size and colour.

There on the counter would be the cause of all my excitement: a long, shapely glass leg upside down on a swivel base. The salesperson wore black horn-rimmed glasses and Mother called her by her first name. She and Mother would decide on the size and colour, and the woman would open the thin box on the counter, fold back the tissue paper, and the two of them would look over the stockings lying flat in the box.

Once they had mutually decided the pair of stockings in front of them was suitable, the woman would lift out the stockings ever so carefully, and gently feed one stocking on the glass leg. Then she would nod in my direction. Having gone through this ritual many times before, the woman knew how much I wanted the job of turning the glass leg. I would put a finger on the chrome base and gently turn it, while Mother and she examined it in detail for flaws. Then the stocking would be gently removed, and the other one put on for inspection. Again, I was given the honour of turning the glass leg ever so slowly.

It was all I could do to restrain myself from giving the chrome base a good rip to see how fast it would go. However, I knew the importance of this job, and realized that if I ever did anything to jeopardize the privilege, it would be the last time Miss Horn-Rimmed Glasses would nod in my direction ever again. Once the stockings were put in a paper bag, wrapped in their own tissue paper, and Mother had paid her fifty-five cents, I would run my hand over the glass leg one more time and give the chrome base a final gentle turn.

I know now, it wasn't the privilege of turning the glass leg, or even that a brand-new pair of silk stockings was coming into our house at a time in which we barely had the money for basic essentials, that intrigued me. It was looking at that long, shapely glass leg, with its beautifully arched ankle and gently curved knee, and knowing that in a few short years, when I grew up, and all things being equal, I would sprout two legs just like it.

Puffed Wheat

I hated puffed wheat passionately. According to my brother Emerson, it was at least better than porridge every morning and it had the benefit of being store bought, but as far as I was concerned it tasted like wood shavings.

It came in a large, white paper bag, covered with a red and blue checked pattern. The top was sealed with string stitching, and I can remember how Mother knew exactly what end of the string to pull to have the whole row of stitches unravel at once. I could never get the closing to cooperate with me.

I ate the puffed wheat even though I hated it. We all ate it. Not because it was something we liked, but because deep inside every bag was buried a kitchen dish or glass. The dishes were white, with deep pink or blue thistles on them. For the longest time the glasses were the colour of amber, what is referred to today as Depression glass. After a few years, the glasses were changed to a pattern that featured red strawberries with green leaves.

We all loved these free gifts that came in the puffed wheat, and that fact kept us assuring Mother that we couldn't imagine our lives without that bowl of cereal in the morning. The company that made and packaged the puffed wheat, however, was most aggravating. The dish or glass was always positioned at the very bottom of the bag. This meant, of course, that we had to eat our way down to the bottom before we reached it. A few times, Emerson tried to dig his hand deep into the bag when

Mother wasn't looking. All he succeeded in doing was sending the cereal all over the table and floor.

Every kitchen I knew in Renfrew County had a big collection of these dishes and glasses. The trick was to get a complete set so that they could be used when company came. We always seemed to have more saucers than cups, dozens of fruit nappies, and many fruit-juice glasses which we rarely used, because we never had fruit juice on the farm.

What we really wanted were big plates and soup bowls. Mother said that we should be grateful for whatever we found in the bag. After all, it was a free gift. Audrey and I both longed for a set of matched dishes, but there was just no way of telling what was in the bag before we bought it. At Briscoe's General Store in Northcote there were always a dozen or so puffed-wheat bags on the floor when we went in to make our purchase, and no amount of squeezing gave us a clue as to what was inside. Mother always let Audrey and I pick out the bag she bought, and we ended up blaming each other if we got still another fruit glass or nappy.

As if this was the most important issue of the decade, Audrey and I discussed the problem at great length when we were in the privacy of our bedroom at night. If we were going to have to eat the hateful stuff, we felt we should at least know what free gift we were going to get when we got to the bottom of the bag. Then one night Audrey sat bolt upright in bed. She had the perfect answer, but wouldn't give me a hint as to what it was. I was known for telling things when I had been sworn to secrecy. All she told me was that I would find out on our very next trip to Briscoe's General Store to buy the bag of puffed wheat.

That day came at the end of the week. Mother was standing at the counter talking to Mrs. Briscoe, and as usual, Audrey and I were dispatched to help fill our order. There was to be a dime's worth of bulk ginger snaps from the big cookie bins and, of course, a bag of the puffed wheat. Audrey beckoned me over to the corner of the store where the bags stood in rows. My sister put her left hand up her right sleeve and pulled out a long knitting needle. She crouched on the floor and inserted the long needle into the bottom part of a bag. She did this three or four times. "It's a glass," she hissed, moving on to the next one. The exercise was repeated until she finally figured she had struck a bag with a plate in it. She carried it over to the counter as I counted out ten gingersnaps.

When we finally worked our way to the bottom of the puffed wheat bag many breakfasts later, there was the plate—the first one of many obtained exactly the same way over the course of the next several months. Audrey and I snickered every time we went to Briscoe's Store and saw all those bags with tiny holes punched in their bottoms. As our dinner plates accumulated, I thought it was just one more example of how clever my sister was.

Sugar Cakes

The few pennies a farm wife was able to squirrel away usually came from selling eggs in town. That money, unless it was needed for something urgent, was hers alone. It didn't matter if the money came from selling chickens or peddling sticky buns, it was still referred to as egg money.

Mother had her steady egg customers in Renfrew to whom she delivered every Saturday morning. This revenue was kept separate from the rest of the scant amount of money Mother kept in her change purse. This was egg money. It was hers to do with as she pleased.

One day in early spring, Mother hit on an idea as to how she could increase her egg money. It had nothing to do with eggs, but had everything to do with maple syrup. We regularly sold syrup to townsfolk. Bottled in jars that once held molasses, honey or store-bought jam, the customers in Renfrew were always thrilled to have it delivered right to their doors.

Mother's idea was that if her customers liked her syrup, they would like maple cakes even more. She carefully boiled the syrup on the back of the Findlay Oval for hours, until it was just the right consistency. Mother would test it often with the big wooden spoon, letting it run back down into the pot. When it was just thick enough, she poured it into old black muffin tins and set them out in the summer kitchen to harden. Of course, we were forbidden to lay as much as a hand on them as they were to add to Mother's egg money. I could tell she had visions of at least several extra dollars filling that little black change purse from her new enterprise.

That first Saturday, as we headed into town for what mother prayed would be a booming day of business, Emerson was put in charge of the maple cakes and Audrey was responsible for the eggs. The back roads cleared early that year, so we were able to take the old Model T. Mother finally found a place to park the car, but it was far from the main street, where we would much rather have been. Since her egg customers were in a residential part of town, she and Audrey would have to walk while Emerson and I sat in the car with the sugar cakes.

There should have been no problem with this arrangement until Emerson spied a young lad he had played ball against. There was always a fierce rivalry between the town and country boys when it came to softball. The young fellow was on a foot-propelled scooter, and he was running up and down the centre of the road. Emerson stuck his head out the window and yelled an obscenity, which today would pass for a mild comment. The lad and the scooter headed for the car. My brother began to see the error of his ways, and whispered to me that he sure would like a run on the scooter. I reminded him he had a fine way of impressing the young Renfrew fellow and that he was probably heading for the car to take a round out of him.

It was then Emerson hit on an idea. He reached back to the cookie tray and took off a few maple cakes. "Smell these," he offered. With suspicion, the young lad pushed the scooter to the side of the car. I couldn't believe my ears when Emerson said he would trade six of the cakes for a ride on the scooter. The boy didn't take more than a few seconds to think about it. He reached in, grabbed the cakes, sat on the fender of the Ford to tuck into the first one, and handed over the handlebars to Emerson. Emerson went like the wind, right down Raglan Street. I figured when Mother found out about the trade, Emerson would be taking his last scoot on anything.

Mother was back to the car before Emerson. I tried to hide the cookie sheet, but she was already reaching in, saying she had talked a few of her egg customers into trying the sugar cakes…"at a nickel a piece too,' she beamed. When she saw that half-empty cookie sheet, and Emerson flying past the car on the scooter, it didn't take her all day to figure out what had happened.

When he came to a halt, his face scarlet from the exertion, Mother, none too gently, shoved him into the back of the car. We headed for Northcote, without even stopping for our weekly treat of sliced bologna and maple cookies.

Emerson sat cowed in the corner of the back seat, and Mother had the gas lever down as far as it would go. There wasn't a thing she could do about the swapped sugar cakes, but Emerson was never again put in charge of anything that had to be traded in Renfrew. I'm not sure if that was more of a treat than a punishment for him. More than once, Emerson lamented that there wasn't much use going all the way into Renfrew if you didn't have a few cents to spend at the Dime Store.

Wishbones

hicken was so much a staple at our table, that it ceased to be
considered a treat. Chicken stew with dumplings was my
favourite, but roast chicken was what we usually had. In whatever form
the fowl came to the table, the bones were picked bare and then the fight
began. Every one of us five children wanted the wishbone. All except my
older sister Audrey who said she was too mature to fight over such nonsense. Unless one of us laid claim to the wishbone before the meal, there
was always a great to-do over ownership.

As was most often the case, Mother came up with a solution. She kept
a little list of who had claimed it the last time, and so each of us had a
chance at a wishbone once in every four meals that chicken was served.

The haggling wasn't to end there. The wishbone had to be thoroughly
dried out, we discovered, or to try to break it was like pulling on a rubber band. So it had to go through a drying process. The ideal drying
method was to hook it on the little curlicues that were part of the deco-
ration on the old kitchen range. These chrome sides on the warming
closet had little decorative holes in them, and we simply hooked the
wishbone through one of them and waited until it was thoroughly dried
out. At any given time, there were always several white wishbones hanging through the chrome of the stovetop that would be taken off just
when someone was ready to wish for something special. We were all
expected to know which wishbone was ours, and to be scrupulously honest about claiming it. However, one day, that all changed.

As often happened, I was going through a stage where I was feeling very sorry for myself. Mother's saying, "Don't you know there is a Depression on?" was starting to take on real meaning for me. I thought our family was particularly hard done by...me especially. Didn't Marguerite have a white fur coat and she was only seven? Didn't my little friend Joyce have an indoor toilet?

One day, while I was sitting in one of my favourite places in our old log house, I began to daydream. I was in the parlour on the horsehair settee with pillows piled at my back and the heat from the stovepipe, which snaked through the room, warming my body. "I wish the Depression was over," I said to myself. "I wish I didn't have to wear hand-me-down clothes. I wish just once I could have brand-new shoes instead of boys' brogues from my cousin in Regina," and my daydreaming for better days went on and on.

Then it hit me. If I wished for those things in earnest, I mean really wished for them, wouldn't they happen? I could see the old kitchen stove from my position in the parlour. There hung all the wishbones, about ten of them, faded white from the heat of the stove. I waited while Mother put on her coat to go out to the milk house. When the summer kitchen door closed behind her, I rushed to the kitchen, took every last wishbone out of the chrome holes and tore back to the parlour. I had to work quickly if I was to get this all in before Mother came back with the little honey pail of milk.

I spread the wishbones out on the settee, methodically made a wish on every last one of them, and cracked them apart. The short ends I tucked under the elastic leg of my bloomers, and the good ends, as we called them, the ones with the barb, I laid out in a row on the settee. Some things I wished for twice...like the indoor toilet. I wasn't going to take any chances on that one.

When I was finished, I rushed to the kitchen and pulled the broken wishbones out of the leg of my bloomers and fed them into the stove. The good ends had to be kept until the wish came true, or the wish would be wasted. I decided the best place to keep them was in my Sunday shoes, so I ran upstairs and poked them into the toe of my black-laced shoes, which I considered only slightly better than the brown boys' brogues. I then sauntered downstairs, putting on what I considered my most innocent look.

The rest of the day went by without anyone noticing the wishbones gone from the stove, but it was at supper time that the whole issue came to a head. Emerson said he wished he could go into Renfrew to see a wrestling match that was coming to the Agricultural Hall. Father said that was highly unlikely, as the talk at Briscoe's General Store on Saturday night was that admission was going to be a dollar, and with three boys and Father all wanting to go, four dollars was just out of the question. When Emerson started to lament, Mother threw in her favourite comment, "Don't you know there is a Depression on?"

Emerson was just starting to say "I wish"…when he stopped and looked over at the stove for his share of the wishbones. He was up from the table in less time than it took to spit. It didn't take long for everyone's eyes to follow him to that corner of the kitchen.

You'd think he had lost part of an arm! He accused my brothers Everett and Earl who, of course, denied everything. He finally zeroed in on me. I put on my most innocent look and kept right on eating. I vowed I had never laid eyes on the wishbones. Emerson said he was going to conduct a systematic search of the entire house. Audrey said for heaven's sake to settle down, they were only wishbones and they didn't work anyway. Emerson reminded her of the time the three boys wished for a cold snap to freeze the Bonnechere for skating, and the next morning the water was as solid as a brick. Audrey said it was a natural progression of the season, whatever that meant.

This cut no ice with Emerson. Those wishbones were in the house somewhere, and by gar he was going to find them if it was the last thing he did. I tried to picture in my mind my black shoes and where I had left them. Emerson was already taking the stairs three at a time.

Well, within seconds…not minutes…he was down the stairs with the spent wishbones in his hand. He told the entire household where he had found them. I fleetingly thought of denying I had done it, but the shoes, which I obviously had left right in the middle of the bedroom floor, were a dead giveaway.

It was easier dealing with Emerson's wrath than it was with the disappointed look in Mother's eyes. Not only had I stolen the wishbones, which was bad enough, but I had lied about the deed, which according to Mother was a cardinal sin, whatever that meant. I figured it was right up there with murder.

I was ushered to bed and it wasn't even dark out. Emerson said I should have been dealt with more severely. Mother said she was the one who handed out punishment, and if she needed his help she would ask for it.

I lay in bed wishing I lived any place but on that farm out in Northcote. Any place but in that old log house and I wished I could replace my hateful brother Emerson with someone who was not mean like he was...I wished...I wished. If I could only lay my hands on another wishbone was my final thought as I drifted off into a troubled sleep.

Confession

Even though Mother had not gone to the Roman Catholic Church since marrying a Lutheran and moving to Renfrew County, we noticed her rosary was never very far away. We kids assumed she was happy being a Lutheran because she was always baking pies or making costumes for something that was going on at the church. That is to say, she seemed happy enough until one day when her first cousin came to visit from Ottawa.

We called her Aunt Lillie Liver behind her back and Aunt Lillian to her face. Lilly was a devout Catholic and her first gift to us children was a small statue of the Virgin Mary, which she insisted was to sit on our dresser in the upstairs hall.

On this one particular visit to the farm, Aunt Lilly kept up a steady barrage of questions aimed at Mother about her involvement in the Lutheran Church. We kids had moved to the other room where we could hear Lilly ranting about things like mortal sin which we had never heard of before.

She then asked Mother when was the last time she had been to confession. We linked confession with owning up to chasing the old gobbler till it dropped, or admitting to having taken the cookie jar to the back shed where we polished off the contents. We certainly never associated our Mother with making a confession. What ever would she have to confess?

As the days went on, we could hear Mother talk to Father about confession, and that for her own peace of mind she might take a run into

Renfrew to visit the priest. Father chewed on his pipe, and said he thought it was all nonsense, and if that crazy Lilly hadn't come out from Ottawa with those far-fetched ideas, Mother would have never given the Catholic Church another thought.

We all knew that once Mother had an idea in her head there was little anyone could do about changing her mind. She decided that she would, in fact, go into Renfrew to the Catholic Church, and we five children could go with her to see what it was like.

The day rolled around when we were to accompany Mother into Renfrew to make this confession. We all loaded ourselves into the car and Father held open the gate for us. Just as we were passing him, he yelled out, "Remember, you are all Lutherans."

Mother drove right to the church. She told us we could go inside and sit quietly in the back pew. The front of the church, as I remember it, was a beautiful jumble of golds and reds and brass. Rows of little candles flickered in the quiet of the altar.

Mother seemed to know exactly what she was doing. In a hushed voice, she said she expected us to behave and that she would be back shortly. With that she vanished around a pillar at the side of the church. After she had been gone several minutes, Emerson said he thought he should take a look to see where she was. He slid his bottom along the polished seat until he had reached the end of the pew. He peeked around the pillar for a time, and slid back to where we were awaiting his comments. "There's a little house back there with curtains all around it, and I think that's where Mother is," he told us.

Finally, after what seemed like a very long time, Mother emerged as quietly as she had disappeared. We saw no great transformation as far as we were concerned. We didn't think the confession had changed her a bit. Audrey had warned us that she wouldn't be surprised if Mother took on the look of the little statue back on the dresser at home that Aunt Lilly had brought. It was the same old face as far as we could see. Mother hummed a bit going home in the car, and stopped at Briscoe's Store at Northcote for a little bag of peppermints for us in the back seat.

Clearly, the whole episode called for another meeting out of earshot of Mother as soon as we got home. Audrey called the group to order, and

149

we rehashed the day's events. Everett, who occasionally surprised us with his reasoning ability, said he had arrived at a conclusion. He said that it was obvious that God did not know Mother had become a Lutheran and that she had gone back to the Catholic Church to have the priest break the news to Him. That bit of logic made perfect sense to the rest of us.

Now that Mother had confessed to the priest that she had been going to the Lutheran Church, everything would be straightened out. Everett added that the next Sunday would tell the tale. If she headed towards Renfrew, we would have what we had heard old Granny Hines call "a divided household."

I was very relieved indeed when the subject of the Roman Catholic Church and confession was not mentioned again. The following Sunday we were all back in the second-from-the-front pew in the little old Lutheran Church in Northcote.

The most relieved person, by far, was Father. I think he knew it was doubtful he could have done a thing about it if Mother had decided she was going back to the Catholic Church. Audrey, however, who was the oldest of us five kids, reasoned it out this way: There was no Catholic Church out at Northcote, so Mother would have no choice but to drive the distance into Renfrew. Going into Renfrew every week for confession could run into money, as it was twelve miles away. Also, reasoned Audrey, although it always seemed as if Mother was the one who made the major decisions in our lives, when you got right down to it, she said, Father pretty well was the boss. Mother could cajole him into just about anything, but Audrey said she was pretty sure switching from Lutheran to Roman Catholic was one issue he wouldn't tolerate. No sir, if you lived in Northcote, you were either United or Lutheran. Being a Catholic was just out of the question!

Flat Fifty a Week

Tommy Roher was a funny little Englishman who came to Canada as a homeboy. He took to the rails in the thirties when he could no longer stand the abuse he had to take from a farmer in another county. When he arrived at our back door one spring day, he had nothing but the clothes on his back.

He was looking for something to eat, and for work. The first request was easy to fill. All he had to do was show that he had clean fingernails. That was how Mother judged a person's character. She always said if someone didn't have enough pride to keep his fingernails clean, she doubted he cared about much else either. Tommy Roher's fingernails were clean, and he was invited to our noon dinner table.

We children thought he talked funny. We had never been face to face with someone from England before. He was just digging into his second piece of pie when he asked Father if there was any work he could do on our farm. Father assured him there was, but that money was as scarce as strawberries in February, and the possibility of our taking on farm help for a salary was pretty remote.

Tommy looked thoughtful and then made a suggestion. He would work for his room and board, a flat fifty of Players cigarettes and perhaps the odd dollar when available. Father and Mother figured that Tommy could perhaps increase the productivity of the farm by five dollars a month. The fifty cents needed weekly for the Players cigarettes could be realized by killing off a few extra chickens every Saturday.

The deal was made. Tommy moved into the back summer kitchen in a corner of the room that Mother curtained off with a piece of wire and creton to give him some privacy. He was a small man and so fitted easily into my brother Earl's overalls. He was given a pair of those and a pair of gum rubbers that had patches on top of patches. He seemed perfectly content with his new wardrobe.

The day after he arrived he asked Father if he could perhaps get his flat fifty of Players before the end of the week. He would sure like a smoke, he said. I had never seen a box of flat fifties, and I was very anxious to view this oddity in lieu of wages that our new hired man was asking for. Father said he thought that could be arranged and that very afternoon I went with him to Briscoe's General Store on the Northcote Side Road to buy the box of cigarettes.

Father had no money, so Mr. Briscoe wrote on a bill that we owed for a box of cigarettes and hung it on our peg. He handed Father a case that was made of pale blue tin and sealed with some sort of a sticker. I told Father I would hold it on the way back to the farm. When I put the box to my nose, the smell was a bit like the pipe tobacco Father made at home. I wanted desperately to look inside but Father wouldn't let me and so I had to content myself just to hold the box until I got back to the farm.

I handed it over to Tommy who was standing at the gate waiting for us. He broke the seal with a thumbnail and opened the thin flat box. There inside were two rows of the smoothest cigarettes I had ever seen. They were not at all like the ones Uncle Alec Thom rolled by hand. These were all the same size and packed perfectly. It was then I discovered they were called flat fifties because not only did they cost fifty cents but also there were exactly fifty cigarettes in the box.

Tommy took one out and lit it with a wooden match. He took out two more and put them in his pocket. I watched him as he went into the summer kitchen and placed the tin box carefully on the windowsill in his corner of the room. He turned and looked in my direction, paused a moment, then took the tin box and put it under the mattress on his cot. I guessed he was removing temptation from my brothers who I'm sure would have no qualms about snaffling a cigarette if the spirit moved them.

By the end of the week, Tommy had used the last cigarette in the tin box. He asked me if I wanted the empty tin. I was thrilled and immediately ran upstairs to tuck it under my mattress, just as Tommy had done when the box was full.

I found all sorts of uses for the boxes in the thirties. They were perfect for holding hair ribbons and small lace hankies. One I kept especially for notes my friend Joyce Francis wrote to me at the Northcote School. Soon there were too many for under my mattress, so I stacked them in neat piles under the bed.

I encouraged Tommy to smoke as fast as he could and I collected the boxes for years. They are gone now. Only the memory remains of those tin boxes and the English homeboy who was content to work for so little in return. At Briscoe's General Store at Northcote, it didn't matter if we had money or not—whatever we needed could always be put on our bill. In this way Tommy was assured of having his flat fifty of Players, three meals a day and place to sleep.

Refuge

Depending on the season, I had two places to which I regularly ran away from home. In the fall it was always the hayloft; in the spring and summer, I always chose the west hill. It was just far enough way from the house that I felt like I was actually leaving home for good. Most importantly, however, I could still see my Mother in the kitchen window, and Father and the boys moving about the barnyard. I was very timid as a child, and felt that even to venture as far as the west hill was just about the bravest thing I ever did.

All sorts of upsets would send me off to the west hill, but usually it was something my brother Emerson had done to me. That would be the cause for me to pack my favourite doll into a brown paper bag, and sneak a lunch into the bowl of my Mother's favourite straw hat. Then off I'd go.

I never told anyone I was leaving, although I would leave plenty of telltale signs. This was just in case someone within the family had a moment of remorse and decided to come looking for me. Heaven forbid that I should spend hours on the west hill, without anyone knowing where I had actually gone.

I think I was the only one in the family to actually run away from home, if you could call going across the Bonnechere and up to the top of the hill running away from home. One of my lasting memories from back in the thirties was that of feeling put upon. This was because I was the youngest in a rowdy family of five and for this reason was given all sorts of chores that none of the others had to do. Mother insisted it was because I was too little to do the heavy chores. Therefore, I had to fill the woodbox, skim the cream, toast the bread on the Findlay Oval, and do countless other little chores which Mother and Father thought I could handle in spite of my skinny frame.

It was this discrimination that sent me off to the west hill one hot summer day. You see, once a week it was my chore to crawl under all the beds in the house with an old piece of well-soaped woollen underwear and dust the floor. Back then, there were no casters on the legs of the beds, and it was impossible to pull them out from the wall. Heaven forbid that the dust from the feather mattresses would not be cleaned up at least once a week.

It was a job I hated with a passion. Mother insisted I was the only one who could fit under the beds. Audrey was too tall, the boys were too big. I was just the right size.

I remember that particular Saturday I was getting ready for this most hateful of jobs. Mother had given me the pail of soapy water and a piece of underwear from the ragbag and I was heading for the stairs. Emerson had antagonized me all morning. He threatened to give my favourite cat to the mailman, he sicked the old gobbler on me when I was gathering eggs, and now he was standing on the bottom step telling me that I would probably have to do under the beds for the rest of my life, since it was obvious to everyone I was never going to grow another inch, ever.

He moved up the stairs behind me, and perched at the top so that he could continue his barbs as I did my hateful chore. I did my best to ignore him. Although I would liked to have done so, I managed to wipe under two beds without throwing the pail of water on him. I knew I would be the one to have to clean up the mess.

I had the job down to a science. I would ring out the cloth before I crawled under, and then reach out for it when I was properly positioned. Emerson had shinnied off the top step as I was just getting ready to slide under the last bed that was in the big hall, which served as the third bedroom upstairs.

After sliding under, I could see his bare feet at the foot of the bed. I did my best to ignore him, and reached for the cloth. Where it should have been, Emerson had put a toad, which he obviously had been hiding down the front of his shirt. It was the slimiest thing I had ever latched onto in my life.

I was out from under the bed like a bolt of lightning. The pail spilled, and before I could land a punch on Emerson, he had taken the steps four at a time and was out the door to the barn.

Unless Mother actually caught someone in a vile act, she wouldn't listen to scrapping between us children over what she called petty arguments. I knew my only recourse was to run away from home. I packed a lunch, took my doll and Mother's straw hat and headed out. There was no one around to see me go, so I made loud coughing sounds all across the field. I sat on the top of the hill on my favourite rock. I could see my house plainly and I gave serious thought to never going back. I knew I would eventually. I always did. But for that special time in my life, the west hill was the best refuge I could find in a cruel world of brothers and household chores.

 156

Stirring the Heart

The essay was simple enough to allow a child who had not yet learned to write, to print her very own thoughts on what made her happy. When the essay came home with my daughter from school, I marvelled at its simplicity, and yet was moved by its impact. In my daughter's childish and bold printing, she had spoken volumes about the delight of enjoying something as ordinary as fresh sheets on her bed, right off the clothesline. Of all the toys that filled the playroom, the new bike with the training wheels, and a cookie jar that was never empty, her heart was stirred most by fresh sheets right off the clothesline!

I have often thought about that child's essay since it was written more than thirty years ago, and have on more than one occasion tried to think of all the things that stir my heart every day. Just getting up each morning to face another day can stir my heart. As most of the world sleeps, I find the greatest joy in moving around the house quietly so as not to disturb those still in bed. On slippered feet I have a ritual that rarely varies. I open the blinds in the living room and look out at the lake we live on, often seeing a blue heron sitting on the dock on one leg. Like me, he is an early riser, and we both share the moment of looking into the mist that surrounds the island.

Statistics are proving that we are an ageing population. Due to the strides made in medical science, it is expected our lifespan is bound to increase. We are already seeing this scenario becoming a reality. There is an ongoing need for more and more facilities for the ageing population, and many are enjoying a good quality of life in spite of their increasing years. To me, it is a joy to spend time with those who are older and much wiser than I am. I have been fortunate to have had the opportunity of visiting many of the retirement centres and care facilities that have sprung up across our country in the past decades. I always come away richer. The residents in these homes are always happy to share their stories, and I am a willing listener. I never cease to be amazed at how much pleasure these very senior people get from the simplest acts of kindness. They delight in showing me a card they received in the mail. They tell me the church they are no longer able to attend has remembered them with a plant or a box of homemade cookies. Each gesture of kindness stirs their heart.

Someone I know has been bedridden for almost twenty years. Allergic to light, she has lived in almost total darkness. She has also lost her ability to walk, to sit for long periods of time, and to see life around her that all of us take for granted.

What she hasn't lost is her boundless joy of life! Her wonderful sense of humour and the happiness she brings to those around her is infectious, and after a visit with her, you come away filled with sheer gratitude and a stirring in your heart.

This final section is all about circumstances and happenings that have stirred the hearts of those in the stories. Even though the stories are of another era, the lessons in them are as up-to-date as your latest electronic invention.

Sounds

The sounds of the 1930s live on long after that era has passed. Now, so many years later, something will trigger a memory of a sound, and my mind reels back to another time and another place. Sounds such as the lament of the whippoorwill, heard only at night, as it nested in the trees. His was a lonesome song, and even now I can remember burrowing deeper into the feather mattress trying to separate myself from his sad lament. He frightened me, and yet on the occasional night when he nestled in a far-off tree, we missed him, and were glad when he came closer to our home. Where have all the whippoorwills gone, I wonder?

I can also remember those early morning sounds in our house before the grey dawn broke, as my father made his way down to the kitchen. Even though he was downstairs, I could follow his routine in my mind's eye, and picture his every move. I could hear papers being scrunched into a ball, and the lids of the Findlay Oval being scraped across the top of the stove. I would hear pieces of kindling being methodically placed on top of the paper. As I lay upstairs I knew that the small sticks would be put together like the rail fences that circled our farm. Then I would hear father lift a log from the woodbox, and I'd listen as the fire started to crackle around the kindling. Soon I would hear the pipes responding with snaps from the heat. I remember dozing off again, with the cosiest of feelings, knowing the night chill would soon be gone from the house.

I believe that nothing these days can replace the wonderful sound of the steam engine whistle as it pulled the freight cars through the Ottawa Valley night. We would hear it faintly in the distance, and by the time the train reached the crossing that ran through our back field, the whistle was clear and sharp. Just as the train left our farm, we would hear two short blasts, and our father would say, "And hello to you too, Tom."

Never again will I hear the plop-plop of the butter churn. I could always tell when the cream was about to turn into butter, because replacing the hollow sound in the churn would be the thud, as the handle and disk hit thickening butter. I can remember not understanding why the cream turned, but I marvelled at the process and loved the sounds my efforts created inside the churn. There isn't much thrill today, I'm afraid, in going to the supermarket and buying a cube of butter if you haven't had a hand in its making.

And those wonderful sounds of the sleigh runners cutting the snow on a crisp winter's night or the wagon wheels grinding out a rhythm on a gravel road. These were sounds that could lull a young child to sleep sitting on her mother's lap.

And what of the frogs croaking in the swamp at night? Is my memory playing tricks on me or do I remember the summer evenings alive with the sounds of the frogs? We used to think we could tell the difference between the old bullfrogs and the young. Do I just imagine that the frogs today seem tired? It's as if they are trying to say, "It's just too much effort."

At the time I would have found no romance in the sound of the old brass, hand-rung school bell, but in my imagination today, I see Miss Crosby come to the top step at the front of the schoolhouse, and I see her pump her hand that holds the heavy brass bell. The sounds ring out loud and clear in my memory, as I see the clapper fall against the inside of the bell. The bell at the top of the schoolhouse was also brass, and in my mind I hear it again.

There are many things I do not miss about the farm during my childhood years. The hard work, which was the lot of my parents, for one. But when I think of the wonderful sounds of those years on the farm, sounds that bring back the feeling of contentment and memories of special happenings, a sadness comes over me, and I long for that which will never return.

Fireflies

I was terrified of the dark. A fear brought about, I am sure, by trips to the outdoor privy in the dead of night. However, at this particular time of the year, and reinforced by the presence of my sister and brothers, nothing could keep me indoors in the evenings.

What took us out were the fireflies. At first I was frightened of them too. Probably because my brother Emerson said each one was an off-spring of the devil and they were out looking for young farm girls to haul away to goodness knows where. My sister Audrey soon put a stop to that hateful rumour.

We would wait until it was pitch-dark. Even though we never went any further than the pump in the yard, I made awfully sure I was within running distance to the kitchen door. We had a row of lilac trees which ran from the gate to the grape arbour, and this is where the fireflies seemed to be in the greatest abundance. The boys ran around like mad dogs, swatting away and, of course, rarely connecting. Conversely, my older and much wiser sister would lead me by the hand to the old wooden swing in the grape arbour, and she would say that if we sat very quietly, the fireflies would come to us.

We had to sit very still, because the old swing had a squeak that Audrey was sure would scare off the fireflies. I huddled close to her and waited patiently for them to come. The vines of the grape arbour hung down low, touching the sides of the swing, and so we would just sit and wait…and watch.

We were contented to do nothing more. The boys, however, evil and mean as they were, would catch the fireflies, pinch them between their fingers and line up the carcasses on their bare arms so that they looked like they were wearing tiny little flashlights. Then they would run through the yard waving their arms like a windmill, and we could see the dots of lights. Audrey and I thought it was a hateful thing to do to the fireflies, but we were powerless to halt the brothers from committing their murderous deed. It didn't help a bit when I told Mother what they were doing, and she replied she suspected just about every boy in Renfrew County was out doing exactly the same thing.

I was never very fond of anything that resembled an insect, and it took a great deal of courage to allow a firefly to light on my hand. Audrey assured me they were harmless, especially since we had no intention of ripping them apart as the brothers did.

Since Audrey had dispelled Emerson's theory that they were messengers on the devil's mission, I wondered just exactly what a firefly was and begged her for an explanation. After all, wasn't she ten years older than me? Surely she must know about things like that.

This was the story my older and much wiser sister created to satisfy my curiosity about fireflies. She said they were pieces of stars that had broken off. On hot nights, when the angels of heaven were looking for something to do, they would leave the farthest reaches of the night sky where they lived, and would seek cooler air by floating down towards earth. To rest, the angels would land on a star, which Audrey explained was very fragile. Little pieces would break off, and they would come tumbling down to the ground. Just before the little pieces of stars landed, they would hitch a ride on the back of a tiny fly to break their fall.

Thereafter, if by chance a firefly touched my arm, I would thrill to the notion of its journey, and marvel that it had travelled millions of miles to get to our farm in Renfrew county. The boys, naturally, thought the story was just about the craziest they had ever heard of, but it was Audrey I chose to listen to and believe. Being older and wiser than the brothers, she was the very one to bring magic into our lives.

Although there aren't nearly as many fireflies today as there were back then, I still wonder if there isn't a bit of truth in Audrey's legend. Could they not be exactly what she said they were? Perhaps they are, in fact, pieces of stars coming down to earth to bring a touch of mystery to our part of the planet. Time may alter many things in our lives, but today, so many years later, I like to think that some of the magic of that special time in my life lives on.

All Dressed Up for Company

For the most part, our everyday lives were simple and uncluttered without the trappings that were common-place for townsfolk. We used a red-checked oilcloth cover on the kitchen table, our cutlery was battered with the fork tines twisted from prying out corks from too many bottles, and dinner napkins were simply unheard of. All of which suited Father just fine. He felt eating a meal was serious business. The main purpose when he sat down at the kitchen table was to say grace, put food in his mouth, chat a bit, but not too much, and then move away to the creton couch for a midday nap. After supper, it was relocate to the rocking chair in front of the Findlay Oval with the *Ottawa Farm Journal.*

Mother, of course, coming from the city and all, would have liked things a little more elegant. She often said her New York friends would be flabbergasted at the lack of niceties, as she put it, that we had to endure on the farm. Father would retort, "Then that's the place for them to stay."

When we had company from Ottawa or Arnprior, Mother, as we would say today, pulled out all the stops. On Sunday morning before church (our company usually came on Sundays), Mother would head for the big round-topped trunk at the top of the stairs. I was always right behind her; I loved the trunk and all the treasures it held.

Here was an array of niceties that mother had brought from New York, to be brought out only when company was expected. First there was the wonderful, long white damask tablecloth. Shiny and always freshly laundered with a bit of starch, it was packed away between the same pieces of white tissue paper Mother had used to bring it in from New York years before. It weighed a ton, I thought then, and packed away with it were twelve serviettes as big as pillow slips. Mother would hand them out to me and I was given the job of seeing that the parcels got down to the kitchen table free from wrinkles. The leaves would already have been added to the big oak table, extending it to seat ten or twelve adults. We younger children always had to eat at another spot in the kitchen, which I thought was grossly unfair.

Mother would fold a big flannelette sheet lengthwise to put over the red plaid oilcloth, and then the white damask cloth would go on top. It was as much as your life was worth to put a finger on the table once it had been set up. When Mother wasn't looking, I would run my fingers over the surface, marvelling at the smooth satiny feel of the damask. If Father happened to be in the house while these preparations for company were going on, he would mutter under his breath, "Nonsense, just plain nonsense." As usual, Mother paid him no heed.

Mother would then go to the old cupboard drawer and take out the rolls of our Sunday-best silverware. I don't suppose it was silver at all, tin more than likely. But it was rolled up in long pieces cut from bleached flour bags. She would unroll these at the work table in the kitchen, and inside would be all these knives, forks and spoons with ivory handles, yellowed with age. Father hated eating with the company silverware. The knife blades were so dull that he would lament, "You couldn't cut butter with these things and the forks have a funny taste off them."

When Mother was finished setting the table for our company, I thought there probably was a very good chance it was the nicest-looking table in all of Renfrew County. I doubted even the rich people in Renfrew could match it. We had to use kitchen dishes, the ones that came in puffed wheat, because we didn't have anything else, but with those beautiful serviettes folded across each plate, the dishes became truly elegant.

Once everyone was seated at the table, Father flatly refused to place the napkin on his lap. Mother would glare at him from the other end of the table, but she could have been in Eganville for all Father cared. There sat the napkin, right through to the end of the meal. It was his way of objecting to all the fuss Mother went to for Sunday company.

From my place over at the second table at the far end of the kitchen, I would look at that lovely table with the single red geranium plunked down in the centre, and I would wonder what all this talk was about a Depression. I thought we were the richest people in all of Canada.

Survival

The *Renfrew Mercury* was our link between our home and the community around us. It came once a week, delivered by the old mailman with horse and cutter in winter and a rattling buggy with a black top in the summer.

The *Mercury* was wrapped in a small piece of brown paper with our name printed on the outside. Father couldn't wait for it to arrive. Our mail came in the mornings, and on the day the *Mercury* was due, Father always made a point of being in the general vicinity of the mailbox. Then he'd pause a mite from whatever he was doing, come into the kitchen, lower himself into the old rocker by the stove, and open the paper as carefully as he would an important legal document.

Without exception, during those lean years of the thirties, his face would take on a look of concern as he scanned the want ads, and I would know that he was reading to see what neighbour was running a notice of a mortgage sale. They were as common as groundhogs in those Depression years. Each week, there would be one or two more that hadn't been there the week before.

Father would read these ads, and his face would take on a sad and thoughtful look, and I know now that he was wondering if some day our farm would be listed as one of those that could hang on no longer. So many farmers had to rely on money borrowed from the bank, putting their farms up for collateral, and then the frantic fight to survive foreclosure took over. A bit of grain sold here, a piece of farm machinery sold there, produce peddled in town to help put staples on the table. And those who had to take out mortgages could never hope to buy things as frivolous as new shoes or a winter coat. Hand-me-downs were recycled and recycled again, until there was nothing left to the garment.

The mortgage sales were like any other auction sale, with farmers coming from miles around. Of course, the banker would be there too, or the wealthy individual who had made the mortgage possible. I can remember my father saying that often the owner of the farm would be nowhere in sight. Even though mortgage sales were as common as winter flu, there was that feeling of failure that sent the debt-ridden farmer into hiding.

We were luckier than most. Although there was little or no money for extras, we survived those Depression years without a mortgage, because Father, as the only son of third-generation German immigrants, had inherited the farm. That didn't mean we were any better off than those around us. It simply meant we were spared the monthly mortgage payment on top of all the other bills that poured into the house on a regular basis. Bills from the grist mill, from the blacksmith, from the hardware store.

A mortgage sale usually meant the farmer was finished. Although one time I recall that a farm was sold close to us and bought by a neighbour who allowed the debt-ridden owner to remain and work the land on a share basis. That didn't happen very often.

I never knew where ousted farmers went, or what they did after their land was sold from under them. Sometimes we saw them on the street in Renfrew, so I reasoned that they had moved into town—a fate, I felt at the time, that would be worse than death itself. Always the mortgage sales were on farms that I scarcely knew. I justified my feelings of indifference by saying I only knew the children from the Northcote School. Father was always very upset when a neighbour from Admaston Township was forced to sell his farm and livestock and farm implements. When he read the ad in the *Renfrew Mercury*, he would be sad for days, and nothing could take him out of his mood. He attacked his chores with a special energy, working late at night and rising before dawn, as if an increase in his workload would be a safeguard from the malady that was striking friends and neighbours in Renfrew County.

Even though there were times when he wondered where the next dollar was coming from, I know that deep in his heart he knew that our farm, through the good fortune of inheritance, would never hit the auction block. Father never for a moment neglected to thank who he considered responsible for our welfare. Each time grace was said at the kitchen table, he prayed loud and long his thanks. Always, after the *Renfrew Mercury* made still another proclamation of a mortgage sale, Father prayed for the unfortunate farmer who was not so blessed.

A New Kind of Worry

Saturday nights were times I cherished as a very young girl. Almost every week, there would be a house party where we children would be bundled up and hauled to a neighbouring farm, or several families would gather in our home for the Saturday-night house party.

If nothing had been planned, then we sat around the big pine kitchen table making our own fun. I liked those family times almost as much as I liked the neighbourhood get-togethers with the old country music, big baskets of sandwiches, and the smell of green tea boiling on the back of the cookstove.

Then, one year, everything changed. Oh, the neighbours still got together, but not with the frequency as in months gone by. There seemed to be a difference about those Saturday-night parties. For the longest time I couldn't put my finger on it, but I knew deep in my soul that something had changed.

There didn't seem to be the merriment any more. The adults would sit around the kitchen for the longest time, and the talk would be about things I had never heard of before. Uncle Alec would yet to have taken his fiddle out of the case, where it rested across his knees. I would see Aunt Bertha looking over at her big strapping sons...a gang of them there was, too. I heard her say, "I don't know what I would do if I lost one of them." I couldn't imagine why Aunt Bertha would ever lose one of her sons. Surely they knew every turn in the Northcote Side Road like the back of their hands.

One night the conversation centred around a neighbour's lad, just barely out of his teens. The talk was that he had gone to the war. I knew this wasn't like a holiday...or a trip to the city...but that it was very serious business. I saw that it caused all the adults great worry and yet I couldn't imagine what they were worried about. Wasn't the war in some far-off place? Wasn't it written in the *Ottawa Farm Journal* that it was happening across the ocean? Imagine a Renfrew County farmboy going off to war! That would never happen out in Northcote!

Even mother, who was a great "clipper" when it came to the newspapers and the few magazines that came into the house, passed up cutting anything out about the war. The big scrapbooks of clippings on happenings as remote as an earthquake in New York continued to grow fat as she cut and pasted. Whenever there was a news story about the war, she would pass over it, and when she was finished reading the *Ottawa Farm Journal* with all the horrible stories in it about the conflict faraway, she would scrunch up the paper into a ball. Instead of it going into the woodbox to start the morning fire, it was fed at once into the kitchen stove. She would stand and watch the flames lick around it, and finally render the dreadful news stories to ashes. It was as if she could rid us all of of the threat of war by burning the stories that brought it ever closer to Renfrew County.

This sombre mood hung over our house and those of our neighbours like a great black cloud. I tried to figure why everyone was so worried about something that was happening so far away. I just could not bring the reality of the war into focus.

We would hear of another young Renfrew County lad going off, and I began to see boys in soldiers' uniforms on the streets in Renfrew. Once we went to the CPR station with a neighbour family and watched tearful goodbyes being said from the platform as the train carried a loved son down the tracks and away from the only home he had ever known. Still I would not admit that the war would ever affect our family out there in Northcote. Surely the war would never come to Canada, and certainly it would never change a thing about our lives.

But of course it did come to Renfrew County. Not actual battles, for which I was grateful; but the long terrible fingers of the war touched just about every family that lived in the tight community I always thought was so safe and removed from any kind of strife. As I saw first one brother, then two, and finally three, come home wearing those strange uniforms, two khaki and one air-force blue, I knew once and for all that the war had finally invaded my safe refuge in Renfrew County.

When one brother, not much more than a young lad, left for overseas and celebrated his seventeenth birthday in Holland, and another went off to Italy, a place he couldn't even find on a map, and the third go to Halifax where he would spend the remainder of the war years, I finally knew why Mother and Father wore the worried looks of war.

There were many anxieties to crowd out happy thoughts in a child's mind during those years. Worries that we would all end up in the County Home. Fear that we would come down with diphtheria and die. But surely the most constant worry for me was that my brothers would not come home to the farm after they had donned their uniforms. I worried that no amount of nightly prayers could save them. I remember our nightly prayers at my mother's knee, now down to just my sister and me, and how, after we had said our final "Amen," I would go to the braided rug beside my bed and ask God to keep them safe and bring every young boy from Renfrew County back home. Of course, only part of that prayer was answered, as grieving parents know too well.

The Exercise

In the late fall a sort of restlessness came over Mother. She talked about her beloved New York City more than at any other time of the year. She watched the late-day sky with an intensity, as if she could ward off the night and the oncoming winter just by wishing them away.

Sometimes she would say to Father, "I love Renfrew County any season but fall and winter." Father was known to retort, "Well, that means you only love it half the time." There was no purpose in Mother's trying to explain.

She kept very busy this time of year. There was the house to get ready for winter. Windows to pack with flour-bag strips, the braided rugs to unroll from under the beds, and the kitchen to shift around so that the old pine table was close to the Findlay Oval. But this never seemed to be enough to keep Mother's mind off faraway places. She said she felt cut off from everyone in the wintertime. She hated it when Father thought it was time to take the wheels off the old Model T and put the car up on blocks of wood in the drive shed. It was a twelve-mile drive into Renfrew. That was a long cold trip with a horse and cutter when the temperature dipped to more than thirty below, as it so often did.

In the late fall, the house was dark by five o'clock. Mother would light the Coleman lamp and several coal-oil lamps as well, to bring some cheer into the kitchen. Father thought that was a total waste of money.

We children were often allowed to stay up a bit later this time of year.

It seemed to us Mother hated to have the long dark night stretch out before her in the quietness of the old log house. Father would take to his bed early. That was the place to be, he would say, when the wind was howling and sleet was pounding against the windows.

After Father would climb the stairs to bed, Mother would invite us five children to the kitchen table. She would take the Eaton's catalogue from the cupboard and place a pad of foolscap paper beside it. This was an exercise we were very familiar with, because it happened several times during the fall. We would gather around her, and she would start at the front of the catalogue and write down all the things she would be ordering. Always she picked the most expensive dresses for herself, Audrey and me. The boys chose the breeks and plaid flannel shirts.

Then we'd come to the candy section. Here were tin pails of chocolates, red, white and green peppermints, and big round suckers wrapped in paper. We'd write down a ton of Christmas candy on the foolscap, and sometimes add unheard of treats like chocolates made in the shape of Santa Claus. No thought was given to the price.

My earliest memories of this exercise had me wondering where the money would come from. Mother would toss aside my questions, and point to something in the toy pages that would have my heart racing. It, too, would be written down on the ever-growing list.

Always, Mother would look at the pages of Dan River prints. Audrey and I would pick out the patterns we would like to have made into blouses. I was fond of mauve. Audrey favoured blue. Mother would write down a piece of each.

She would be filled with excitement, and when that happened she would get two rosy spots on her cheeks. I used to think she was the prettiest woman in the whole of Renfrew County. When we had gone through the catalogue from front to back, and all our choices had been made and written down on the foolscap pad, Mother would put down the pencil and breathe the biggest sigh as if to say, "There, that's done with." We would then be hustled upstairs to get ready for bed and to say our prayers with Mother.

In that old log house, with its paper-thin walls, every sound was familiar. I could hear Mother go back downstairs and shake the grates of the stove. I remember hearing the sound of her filling the wash basin with water in case the pump froze overnight. Then I would wait for the sound that I knew would be coming next. I would hear Mother rip the sheet from the foolscap pad and scrunch it up in her hand. Next would be the sounds of the stove lid being scraped across the top of the stove, and I knew the paper in her hand, with all the things we listed from the Eaton's catalogue, was being fed onto the hot coals.

The next morning there wouldn't be a sign of the previous night's activity. The catalogue and the pad would be back in their place in the cupboard. None of us mentioned the evening before. For a time, I knew, Mother's thoughts of New York and her feelings of loneliness would be gone. Just like the make-believe order from the Eaton's catalogue.

A Northcote Winter

*I*t doesn't take much for a memory to be triggered in my mind. A walk along our country road and the smell of burning wood tumbling from a chimney along the way causes my mind to flash back to those days in the thirties when our very survival depended on the cookstove in the kitchen.

If I close my eyes I can see Father plugging the woodbox with logs. The smells of burning cedar and spruce fill my nostrils. Or I see Mother on the coldest day of the winter with the perspiration pouring off her face as she laboured over a steaming pot of potatoes with the masher, or hauled bubbling pies from the oven.

The very smell of the fires along our country road remind me so much of that time in my life when the Findlay Oval, the only source of heat in the entire house, served so many purposes. It radiated heat through a network of pipes that snaked through the rooms upstairs. A fine piece of chicken wire, which hung over the warming closet, dried our wet mitts and hats. A block of wood between the Findlay Oval and the back wall of the kitchen served as a resting place for the felt inner soles from our gum rubbers. The opened oven door would hold a creton cushion that provided a cozy resting place for Father's stockinged feet as he read the *Ottawa Farm Journal* after supper at night.

Then I pass barns along this country road of today and I smell the scent of the horses in the enclosure, and my mind careens back more than sixty years. A jumble of wonderful warm memories come tumbling out. I think of bright nights when Father would hitch up the flat-bottomed sleigh, and with a bale of hay to rest our backs against, we would head across the fields, impassable in the summer, to our neighbours' for an evening of cards and music. I barely have to stretch my mind to bring up the sounds of the runners of the sleighs crunching along on the hard snow, and the soft clopping of the horses' feet as they searched out a path. How I loved the moonlit night and the ride across that twenty-acre field. We always played a game where we tried to count the stars, and sometimes we saw a shooting star which Mother always took as a sign of bad luck. Father said that was sheer nonsense, which took my fear away immediately.

I especially liked the moonlit ride coming home if the Montreal cousins were with us. Bricks would be burning hot from sitting out the evening on the neighbours' cookstove. They would be wrapped in grain bags or newspaper and placed at our feet for the ride back over the big field. Mother always sat with her arms around young Terry and me. Ronny considered himself much too grown-up to be held, preferring to be at the back of the sleigh with my brothers. By the time we pulled into the yard in front of our old log house, little Terry would be fast asleep and would have to be carried inside. The next morning he would vow he had been awake all the time.

Then if I go further up our country road to the little bridge, I don't see McGibbons Creek, I see the Bonnechere River. My memory of skating on a cleared block of ice fills me with a warmth that defies the cold of the day. I think of sitting on the fallen tree, and how patient my sister Audrey was as she tied and retied my skates until they were just right. Because I was the youngest, I was on the very end of the line for crack the whip. Today I can still feel the sharp wind on my face as we cut across the Bonnechere, laughing, falling, licking the snow off our mitts, cozy warm, in oversized hand-me-down melton cloth snowsuits.

If I scrunch my eyes up tight, I see my mother in the kitchen waiting for us to come home with steaming hot chocolate in a white granite pot on the back of the stove, and ginger cookies for dipping. I see all of us sitting around the big pine table, in nothing but our long underwear, with no embarrassment. My older sister Audrey, my brothers and any number of neighbourhood children who had tagged along, would be laughing and reliving the day while our clothes dried out on chairs around the stovepipe.

Today I see a young mother pulling her child in a brightly coloured plastic sleigh and I think of the homemade sleigh we loved. Father spent hours on it, getting the runners just right. I hope I can be forgiven for thinking the sleigh of my childhood was nicer. The smells and the sounds of winter today are like stepping stones, taking me back to another era...when the cares of the world belonged to someone else. Once again I feel content, wrapped in the warmth of another time.

Introducing...
Radio Stories
by Mary Cook

I invite you to look for my next book which will be a bit of a departure in content from my current works, including *Liar, Liar, Pants on Fire!*, *Christmas with Mary Cook*, *Another Place at the Table* and *In My Mind's Eye*.

Radio Stories will be a book about the people I have met along my road as a writer and broadcaster, and who have helped shape my life. I hope I can do justice to their stories, because I would like to share with you the philosophies of others who have left me emotionally richer. I will introduce you to people who have overcome unbelievable odds. You will meet people who have found sheer joy in the most simple of pleasures. I will take you into the secret passages of some of their minds to find out what makes them laugh, and how they have been able to find joy and contentment in spite of terrible hardships.

During my broadcasting career, I have been honoured to win seven Actra awards for these stories. It will be my pleasure to share these stories—and these exceptional personalities—with you.

Look for Radio Stories in 2003

Pig

Exotic woods. What could that mean? Well, to a person seeking out interesting stories and people, it meant turning off the highway and down a long driveway to find out.

I rapped on the door of a spanking new, board house...crafted perhaps with the same "exotic wood" advertised at the roadside. The man who answered the door wore a rakish cap and tweed jacket with leather elbow patches. He wasn't tall, but he gave the impression of being powerful. Jack Semlar thrust out a hand which I immediately noticed was missing a few fingers. When I told him I was interested in doing a story on his business of importing and selling specialty woods, he graciously invited me into his office at the front of his house, which I noted was panelled with beautiful, honey-coloured wood.

Jack had a heavy European accent, and when he said, "Watch the peeg," I had no idea what he was saying. That is, until I looked in the direction he was pointing, right into the decidedly unfriendly eyes of an enormous black and pink pig. Even my life on the farm as a little girl did little to quell the mounting fear I felt towards this animal that, to me, should have been outside rolling in the mud...and not in Jack Semlar's office!

Jack seemed nonplussed at my apprehension over his house guest, and assured me that Pig was as gentle as a lamb. That was the animal's name. Just plain Pig. Nothing fancy. I soon realized there was a better story here than the one about exotic woods.

180

While scratching a now-contented Pig behind the ears, Jack told me how he had come to have this farm animal living in his house. It seems he was delivering a load of wood to a farm near Brockville. The farmer had a piggery, and amongst the litter of newborns was one that looked very much like it would never see the light of another day. "It was scrawny, could hardly stand up, and kept getting routed out of its feeding spot on the mother sow," Jack said. The farmer agreed with Jack that it was unlikely this runt of the litter would last much longer.

Jack Semlar asked for and was given the pig, which he brought back with him to his farm and lumberyard just outside of Perth, Ontario. Pig settled in as if she had been born in the kitchen. She took over a spot behind the cookstove, and thrived on whatever it was Jack fed her.

For some reason Jack was never able to explain, he just didn't get around to moving Pig to the barn. She swam in the swimming pool with Jack's two dogs, and generally did whatever they did, which included running the fields and coming back to Jack when they were called. She was growing fast. No longer was Pig the little runt Jack had rescued from almost-certain death. The Landrace pig was now a whopping 274 pounds, with the beautiful pink and black markings of a prized swine.

Jack adored Pig, and Pig obviously adored Jack. The only problem that had developed was Pig's insane jealousy of anyone who came near Jack or intruded on her territory in the house. Thus Pig's look of malice when I entered Jack's office.

It was obvious to me that this was no ordinary pig. She was as smart as a whip, and Jack maintained that pigs are just about the smartest farm animal there is. And as for being dirty? Don't you believe it!

Pig went everywhere with Jack. He had a big red, four-door Cadillac, from which he had removed the back seat. All Jack had to do was rattle the keys and Pig was at the ready. She would climb into the cavity where the back seat had been, sit on her haunches and gaze out at the scenery, as she and Jack went cruising through the countryside. It was one of these excursions that almost cost Jack his license, and caused a minor mishap on the streets of Perth.

Jack had stopped abreast of another car at a traffic light. The woman driving the other vehicle happened to glance out her window...right into the grinning face of Pig. She became so rattled she put her foot to the floor and clipped off a pole at the side of the road. Jack was ordered to keep Pig at home.

That ban didn't come into effect before I had a chance to display Pig at a public function in the nation's capital, however. We were taking our CBC show to one of Ottawa's more elite shopping locations—240 Sparks Street. I thought it would be great fun to have Pig as a special guest.

There was a ban against transporting domestic animals through the City of Ottawa, and we had to get police permission and an escort to carry out our plan. Jack and Pig drove up in style to 240 Sparks Street, and the throngs there to greet them made all the effort worthwhile.

Pig had been prettied up for the occasion. She had had a bath and was glistening like silk. Jack had tied a wide pink ribbon around her neck, and she didn't seem to mind the leash he used to get her into the rotunda of the complex. The maintenance staff had been warned that a pig would be part of the remote broadcast, and they were there with short brooms and dustpans, waiting for what they were sure would be an inevitable mess. They underestimated Pig—she was completely housebroken. When the show was over, there wasn't as much as a straw in evidence to indicate that she had been there.

Everyone loved Pig. They patted her, hugged her, and fed her muffins and donuts. She was in her glory. She performed the few tricks she had learned, including shaking hands with her front leg, and sitting down on her haunches when she was told. Pig was a hit, Jack Semlar was proud, and I was relieved that my gamble for a unique show had paid off.

It was obvious that Pig was out of the ordinary. In many ways. She even learned to open the door at Jack's house by wrapping that big jaw around the doorknob so that she could come and go as she pleased.

Alas, according to Jack, Pig grew into a hopeless alcoholic. And it was all because of her love of fermented apples. Jack had several apple trees in his yard, and for some reason, Pig preferred to eat them in the dead of night rather than in broad daylight.

One fall night, Pig let herself out of the house and filled her belly with the fermented apples that had fallen from the trees and lay rotting on the ground. She must have had a good feed, because it was assumed later that she had eaten enough to get roary-eyed drunk. She wandered out onto Highway 7, lay down in the middle of the road, and an eighteen-wheeler did the rest.

It was the end of Pig. We all mourned the loss of a very special animal, who thought like a human, lived like a queen, figured she was a dog, and possessed the very human emotion of jealousy.

The Actra award I won for the initial interview with Jack Semlar should have gone to Pig, because she was the true star of the program. Years later, people who either heard that first interview or attended the remote broadcast still talk about Pig. They come up to me and say, "Mind the time you had that pig on your show? Whatever became of her?" And with a sadness I never thought I would feel for a pig, I tell the story of a farm animal that earned the right to live in a human environment.

Also by Mary Cook

Liar, Liar, Pants on Fire! transports readers again to a time when families and communities were bound together by the need to survive. These were tough times for the Haneman family, but Mary Cook's remembrances of growing up on the family farm in the Depression years include even larger servings of joy and laughter.

0-921165-40-4 $16.95

Christmas with Mary Cook is a collection of mary's most requested yuletide stories and recipes. From Pork Tourtières and Old-Fashioned Christmas Fruitcake to short stories that include "The Doll" and "December Birthday," this special edition is sure to warm winter hearts everywhere.

0-921165-51-X $15.00

In 1911, thirteen-year-old Mabel Ernestine Lapointe ran from the heartache of her life in an Ottawa tenement house, and set off on a journey that took her to the giddy heights of New York City. Tragic circumstances forced her return to Canada, to a desolate farm in Renfrew County during the Depression years—a place from which she longed to escape. *Another Place at the Table* is Mabel's story and the story of the farmer who became her husband, offering the young widow and her two children the only sanctuary they could hope for.

This is CBC radio broadcaster, author and storyteller Mary (Haneman) Cook's tribute to the remarkable woman who was her mother.

0-921165-57-9 $16.95

Available from Creative Bound Inc.
1-800-287-8610
(613) 831-3641 (Ottawa)
www.creativebound.com